The USA is Lesterland

Lawrence Lessig

ISBN: 978-1494701604

10 9 8 7 6 5 4 3 2 1

for (my) love,
Bettina

Table of Contents

Preface

In this book, I offer a simple way to understand the nature of the corruption that is the United States Congress today. I also sketch a strategy to fix it. That corruption isn't illegal corruption. It's not the bad behavior of bad souls. It is instead the ordinary behavior of good souls within a corrupted system. It's *legal* corruption, and it has infected and poisoned our government.

Like a magnet beside a compass, or molasses in a gearbox, or a wheel not aligned: This is a system of influence that corrupts the government of our Republic. And it is a bi-partisan, equal opportunity corruption. It blocks the Left. It blocks the Right. It blocks both in the sense that it makes it harder (maybe impossible) for either side to get the principled reform that each side would push.

We all know this. But we've ignored it for too long. For the good of the Republic, for the future we give to our kids, it is time for us to act and fix it.

This book is a companion to my TED Talk, "Citizens." It parallels that talk and builds upon it. Watch the talk first (you can see it at *bit.ly/Lesterland*), then read on for a fuller picture of how we can fix this corruption.

One note on format: Throughout the notes are links to resources on the web. Those links were live as of March 25, 2013. But as links on the Web are highly unstable, we have built a site with all the links archived. If you have any trouble with the links in this book, you can find the archive by the link number at *lesterland.lessig.org*.

One note on form: If you have any comments or reactions you'd like to share, please email me at *comments@lessig.org*. I'm also grateful for corrections. I'm a big believer in sentence fragments, and apologize if that troubles you. But I'm happy to receive suggestions about how to make this argument clear. Thank you in advance.

One final note on freedoms: This work is licensed under a Creative Commons Attribution license (CC-BY-NC (4.0)). That license gives you the freedom to copy, distribute, sell, remix, publicly perform — you name it, whatever rights copyright grants us, you can exercise freely, *so long as* you maintain attribution to this work and your use is "not primarily intended for or directed towards commercial advantage or monetary compensation." (I am asking the original publisher of the ebook, TED Books, for permission to release the work more freely. Check back at *lesterland.lessig.org* for updates.)

A DRM-free PDF of this book is available at *lesterland.lessig.org*. Share freely. And for copyright geeks, you can view the license at *bit.ly/CC-BYNC4*.

Chapter 1:
Lesterland

Once upon a time, there was a place called "Lesterland." Lesterland was a lot like the United States. Like the United States, it had a population of about 311 million souls. Of that, like the United States, about 150,000 were named "Lester."

Lesters in Lesterland had a very important power. There were two elections every election cycle in Lesterland – a general election and a "Lester election." In the general election, all citizens got to vote. In the Lester election, only the "Lesters" got to vote.[1]

But here's the catch: To run in the general election, you had to do extremely well in the Lester election. You didn't necessarily have to win, but you had to do extremely well. Democracy in Lesterland was thus a two-step dance. Lesters controlled the first step.

What can we say about "democracy" in Lesterland?

First, we could say, as the United States Supreme Court said in its remarkable ruling in *Citizens United* v. *FEC*,[2] that "the people have the ultimate influence over elected officials" – for, after all, there is a general election. But the people have that influence only after the Lesters have had their way with the candidates who wish to run in that general election. The people's influence is ultimate, but it is not exclusive. Instead, the field of possible candidates has been narrowed to the field of Lester-plausible candidates, just as the field of candidates that citizens in the Soviet Union could select among had been narrowed by the choices of the Communist Party.

Second, and obviously, this primary dependence upon the Lesters would produce a subtle, understated, and somewhat camouflaged bending to keep the Lesters happy. All candidates, both prospective and already successful, would know that they couldn't gain or retain power without Lester support. Such bending, however, couldn't be too obvious, for fear that it would trigger the votes of voters who resented the Lesters' influence. (No doubt, there were some.) But neither could it be too subtle, for fear that the Lesters would miss who their real allies were. Thus the Goldilocks principle of Lesterland politics: Not too little, and not too much. The best politicians were the best precisely because they practiced this balance well.

Lesterland is thus a democracy, but it is a democracy with two dependences. The first is a dependence upon the Lesters. The second is a dependence upon the citizens. Competing dependences, possibly conflicting dependences, depending upon who the Lesters are.

That's Lesterland.

There are three things to see now that you've seen the democracy called "Lesterland."

(1) The United States is Lesterland.

Like Lesterland, the United States also has 311 million souls. It also has about 150,000 people named "Lester." And it also has two types of elections: One, the traditional "voting election," where citizens cast ballots; the other, a distinctively modern "money election," in which the relevant "funders" give money to afford candidates the chance to run effectively.

The voting elections are discrete — they happen on a particular day, in a regular cycle. They include the vote in the general election; for a small portion of us, they also include the vote in the primary. In both cases, every citizen (save felons) 18 and older has the right to participate. And as the constitution has been interpreted, every citizen (again, except felons) has the right to participate equally. If the vote I cast for my representative to Congress is weighted more than yours (because there are fewer voters in my district than in yours), the Constitution requires the state to redraw that congressional boundary. Equality is thus the norm.

By contrast, the money elections are not discrete. They are continuous. Every day, throughout the election cycle, every citizen is asked to contribute to one candidate or to another. That contribution is in effect a "vote" for that one candidate or the other. But unlike "votes" in the discrete elections, to vote for one candidate in the money election does not mean you can't vote for another as well. Citizens are free to hedge their *money votes* in the money election by voting for both candidates in a two-person race, or as many candidates in as many races as they wish. The only regulation is that no citizen is permitted to give more than $2,600 to any one federal candidate per election, or more than $123,200 to all federal candidates and federal PACs combined in a biennial election cycle.

Finally, and obviously, while the Constitution has been interpreted to require equality in the voting election, there is nothing close to equality in the money election. The per capita influence of the top 1 percent of American voters is more than 10 times the per capita influence of the bottom 99 percent.[3]

As in Lesterland, the money election and the voting election have a special relationship in U.S.A.-land too: To be able to run in the voting election, one must do extremely well in the money election. One doesn't necessarily have to win — though 84 percent of the House candidates and 67 percent of the Senate candidates with more money than their opponents did in fact win in 2012[4] — but you must do extremely well. The average amount raised by winning Senate candidates was $10.4 million; losing candidates raised $7.7 million. The average amount raised by winning House candidates was $1.6 million; losing candidates raised $774,000. Money certainly isn't the only thing that matters. But anything other than money is way, way down the list of "things that matter."

But here is the key to the link between Lesterland and the United States: There are just as few relevant "Funders" in U.S.A.-land as there are "Lesters" in Lesterland.

"Really," you say?

Yes, really. Here are the numbers from 2010:[5]

In the two years that comprised that election cycle, 0.26 percent of Americans gave $200 or more to any congressional candidate. That's 809,229 Americans, just one-quarter of one percent of us.

But the number who gave at least the maximum amount to any federal candidate was just 0.05 percent — that's one-twentieth of one percent, or one person in 2,000, or about 150,000 Americans.

It gets worse. Only 0.01 percent – the one percent of the one percent – gave $10,000 or more to any combination of federal candidates.

A mere 0.00024 percent – roughly 750 Americans – gave $100,000 or more to any combination of federal candidates.

And though my focus in this book is Congress, here's just one statistic from the 2012 presidential election: 0.000032 percent – or 99 Americans – gave 60 percent of the individual SuperPAC money spent in the 2012 cycle.[6]

So along this range – $200+ (0.26 percent), $2,400 (0.05 percent), $10,000 (0.01 percent) or $100,000 (0.00024 percent) – it's hard to believe that someone giving just $200 is a "relevant funder." It's easy to believe that someone giving $100,000 is a "relevant funder." But, conservatively, it is certainly fair to believe that a "relevant funder" is someone giving at least the maximum amount to at least one campaign. So that means just 150,000 Americans, or 0.05 percent of America, or just about the same number of Americans as are named "Lester," are the relevant "funders" of elections in U.S.A.-land. In this sense, "the Funders" are our "Lesters."

So what we can say about "democracy in the U.S.A.," following the lines we drew describing "democracy in Lesterland"?

First, as in Lesterland, we can say, as the Supreme Court said in *Citizens United*, again, "the people have the ultimate influence over elected officials." For again, there is a voting election. But "the people" have that influence only after "the Funders" have had their way with the candidates who wish to run in the voting election. The people's influence is ultimate. But it is not exclusive. Instead, the field of possible candidates has been narrowed to the field of Funder-plausible candidates. If you can't please the Funders, you're unlikely to get a chance to please the voters.[7]

Second, and again as in Lesterland, this primary dependence upon the Funders will produce a subtle, understated, and, we might expect, camouflaged bending to keep the Funders happy. Members of Congress and candidates for Congress spend anywhere from 30 percent to 70 percent of their time raising money to get back to Congress or to get their party back into power.

Thirty percent to seventy percent.

Those numbers are hard to believe, and of course we don't know precisely how members of Congress spend their time because they — unlike us (or at least us lawyers) — don't have to keep time sheets. But if you survey all the studies that have tried to estimate this number,[8] that range is certainly fair. I've been told by some that it underestimates the actual time that is focused on raising money. I've been told by others that many get away with spending much less time.

Still, if you're skeptical about academics' estimates, then the Democrats have at least given us a fairly clear sense of the time that they expect at least the freshman class of the 2013 Congress to spend raising money. As the Huffington Post reported, in December 2012 the Democratic Congressional Campaign Committee gave each freshman a "Model Daily Schedule" that they were to keep. They were told that the leadership expected them to abide by this schedule. This was the schedule:

MODEL DAILY SCHEDULE - DC

☑ 4 hours	Call Time
☑ 1-2 hours	Constituent Visits
☑ 2 hours*	Committee/Floor
☑ 1 hour	Strategic Outreach Breakfasts, Meet & Greets, Press
☑ 1 hour	Recharge Time

"Call time" is fundraising time. So at the very least, these freshman members are told to spend 44 percent of their day raising money. That number is higher if any of the "meet and greet" time is actually effectively fundraising. And that number doesn't even include evenings, which for many members, at least while in Washington, is just more fundraising.

So be conservative about this: Let's round down to just 40 percent. Here, then, is the obvious question:

What does spending 40 percent of your day dialing for dollars from the tiniest fraction of the 1 percent do to human beings, or at least, members of Congress?

How does it affect them? As they develop, over months and months of experience, the skills necessary to flip an unknown Lester on the other end of a telephone to contribute $1,000, or $5,000, how does it change the way they view the world? Or, more important, how does it affect the relevant issues that they, as members of Congress, need to pursue?

It doesn't take a Ph.D. in psychology to recognize the effects of such conditioning. As any of us would, members of Congress who spend hundreds of hours fundraising develop a sixth sense — a constant awareness of how what they do might affect their ability to raise money. They become, in the words of the X Files, shape-shifters, as they constantly adjust their views in light of what they know will help them to raise money. Not on issues 1 to 10, but on issues 11 to 1,000. Leslie Byrne, a Democrat from Virginia, recounted that when she went to Congress she was told by a colleague, "Lean to the green." Then, to clarify, she went on, "[H]e wasn't an environmentalist."[9]

Think of a rat in a "Skinner box" — the device invented by B.F. Skinner, to test whether animals could be conditioned to behave through a system of selective rewards — after the rat learns when to push the buttons it needs to push to get its pellets of food: How is that rat different after it learns that sequence compared to before it learns that sequence? How is the modern American congressman like that rat?

My point is to emphasize the effect that this life has on the character and the attitudes of the congresspeople we put into this fundraising maze: How are they sensitized by this constant need to raise money from the tiniest slice of the 1 percent? How are their judgments affected? No doubt, once or twice every two years these congresspeople face the test of a discrete election — the voting election. That discipline has an effect on them too. But what about the effect of this continuous election? The "money election"? How should we calibrate that?

It's not difficult to imagine what the framers of our Constitution would have thought about this discipline. Or at least, what Madison would have thought. James Madison was likely the most astute of the drafters of our original constitution. He was also its most lucid defender. He (with Alexander Hamilton and John Jay) famously penned a series of pseudonymous essays published at the time the constitution was being ratified — what we today call the Federalist Papers. Those essays tried to explain to the American people why the People should trust this new Constitution and the Republic it promised.

At the core of Madison's thought was the sense of what it meant for a government, or for any branch of a government, to be properly "independent." But to understand what Madison was saying, we have to be careful to understand what his words meant then.

"Independence" for Madison, and for the framers generally, didn't mean that a government, or a branch of government, was free to do whatever it wanted. "Independence" meant instead that the government, or that branch of government, was properly dependent.

An "independent judiciary," for example, is not a judiciary that can do whatever the hell it wants. It is instead a judiciary that is "dependent upon the law" and nothing else. It would be a corruption of a judiciary for its judges to be dependent upon politics as well as the law — as some say the judges in Japan are, because they are moved to remote courts if they rule too frequently against the government.[10] An independent judiciary instead is to be insulated from politics, as a way to reinforce its dependence upon the law.

Madison was keen throughout the Federalist Papers to prove that Congress, unlike the British Parliament, would, under the new constitution, be "independent." And again he demonstrated that independence by showing his readers the ways Congress would be properly dependent. That dependence was different for the Senate than for the House, at least originally. The Senate was selected by state legislatures. It was thus designed to make it properly dependent upon the States.

But the House, as Madison described in Federalist 52, was to be "dependent on the people alone." And among the innovations that Madison was most proud of to secure that dependence "on the people alone" was frequent and regular elections. "Frequent elections," Madison wrote, "are unquestionably the only policy [that can secure] an immediate dependence on, and an intimate sympathy with, the people."[11] And by "frequent," Madison meant "freely by the whole body of the people, every second year."[12]

So if an election every two years was "the only policy" that could effectively secure "dependence" in Madison's view, what would he have thought about an election every day? Or of an election every single time a Congress member votes one way or the other? Or of the election that happens during the four-hour "call time" a representative is to do each day (again, twice as much as is to be devoted to the work of Congress, "committee/floor" time), during which the work of that representative gets measured by the Funders, and the Funders decide whether to support it or not?

Of course, in 1787 such a perpetual election was unimaginable. It took George Washington 10 days to travel from Philadelphia to Cambridge to take command of the Continental Army.[13] Perpetual elections in such a world would be a fantasy. But if we could bring James Madison back to life and ask him what he thought about the innovation within our modern system — of this, perpetual "dependence" — that ratcheted up his innovation of the biannual election, I suspect his first question would be, "upon whom are these representatives perpetually dependent?"

The answer to that question is not the answer that Madison would want — "on the people alone." For the system that we have allowed to evolve keeps Congress perpetually dependent upon "the Funders," while only biannually dependent upon "the People." We have, in other words, allowed a second dependence to seep into the system, a second dependence that puts pressure upon the exclusive dependence that Madison intended — a "dependence on the people alone."

Thus are they dependent, Mr. Madison, upon the Funders. But "the Funders" are not "the People."[14]

So here again, as with Lesterland, we have "a democracy." As in Lesterland, the representatives within that democracy are dependent upon both "the People" and "the Funders" — a competing dependence, and possibly a conflicting dependence, depending upon who "the Funders" are.

Thus, point one:

(1) The United States is Lesterland.

[1]For those worried about the details, imagine that the power is given to people named Lester as of a certain date, one year before Lesterland was founded. And to deal with the sad fact that Lesters die, imagine that each family with a parent named Lester could qualify one of its children, male or female, as a Lester, with all the privileges that Lesterdom entails. By "directly related," Lesterland limits the franchise to people named Lester, married to people named Lester, the children (over 18) of people named Lester, and the parents of a person named Lester. Assume the average number of people "directly related" to a Lester is four. So while Lesters make up only 0.05 percent of the population of Lesterland, those entitled to vote in the Lester election constitute about 0.25 percent of the total population.

[2]558 U.S. 310 ___ (2010) (slip. op., at 44), accessed March 25, 2012 (link #0).

[3]Calculation of Professor Paul Jorgensen, University of Texas-Pan American, on file with author.

[4]B. Bowie and A. Lioz, *Billion-Dollar Democracy: The Unprecedented Role of Money in the 2012 Elections* (New York: Dēmos and U.S. PIRG Education Fund, January 2013), 18, accessed March 25, 2013 (link #1).

[5]"Donor Demographics," 2010, OpenSecrets-.org, The Center for Responsive Politics, accessed March 25, 2013 (link #2). As my focus is Congress, I have used the numbers from the most recent congressional election. The number of Lesters giving money to congressional candidates in 2012 is even lower.

[6]In the TED Talk, I was relying upon older data. The updated number – 99 Americans – is calculated in *Billion-Dollar Democracy* (p. 30; see note 4 above; link #1).

[7]The most obvious earlier parallel to Lesterland in U.S. history is the "white primaries" that dominated some states in the South until the early part of the 20th century. Under those systems, the "private" Democratic Party held a primary to determine which candidate would represent the Democratic Party in the general election. Those private primaries were restricted to whites only. At first the primaries were restricted explicitly, by law. The Supreme Court struck those laws down. See, e.g., *Nixon* v. *Herndon*, 273 U.S. 536 (1927), *Nixon* v. *Condon*, 286 U.S. 73 (1932). In response to these cases, states worked hard to privatize the primaries enough so that the state could not be held responsible for the discrimination against blacks under the Fourteenth Amendment. At first, the Supreme Court upheld these privately discriminatory white primaries, *see Grovey* v. *Townsend*, 295 U.S. 45 (1935). But in *United States* v. *Classic*, 313 U.S. 299 (1941), the Court imposed constitutional requirements on primaries, independent of any state action. The Court recognized that the states in the South had effectively changed "the mode of choice from a single step, a general election, to two, of which the first is the choice at a primary of those candidates from whom, as a second step, the representative in Congress is to be chosen at the election." 313 U.S. at 324 That separation made candidates for Congress no longer dependent upon the people alone, but also, and separately, dependent upon white voters. Both elections thus must be tested by the con-

stitutional norms. That permitted the Court in *Classic* to uphold a private conspiracy to deny a right to vote, and eventually in *Smith* v. *Allwright*, 321 U.S. 649 (1944), to strike the white primary, whether private or not.

[8]L. Lessig, *Republic, Lost: How Money Corrupts Congress – and a Plan to Stop It* (New York: Twelve, 2011), 138.

[9]M. Schram, *Speaking Freely: Former Members of Congress Talk about Money in Politics* (Washington, D.C.: Center for Responsive Politics, 1995), 12.

[10]L. Lessig, *Republic, Lost*, 228.

[11]Z.S. Brugman, "The Bipartisan Promise of 1776: The Republican Form and Its Manner of Election" (paper, Social Science Research Network, 2012), 30, accessed March 25, 2013 (link #3).

[12]J. Madison, The Federalist No. 41, "General View of the Powers Conferred by the Constitution," Independent Journal, from the Project Gutenberg Etext, accessed March 25, 2013 (link #4).

[13]E. Risch, *Supplying Washington's Army* (Washington, D.C.: Center of Military History, U.S. Army, 1981), 64, accessed March 25, 2013 (link #5).

[14]As Dēmos reports, citing a study funded by the Joyce Foundation, "large donors are significantly more conservative than the general public on economic matters." Bowie and Lioz, *Billion-Dollar Democracy*, 15 (see note 4 above; link #1).

In 1996, according to the study, 81 percent of those who gave $200 or more had family incomes greater than $100,000, making them richer than 95 percent of America. Ninety-five percent of contributors were white, and 80 percent were men. Ibid.

Chapter 2:
Worse

Point one was bad. Point two is worse:

(2) The United States is worse than Lesterland.

One could imagine that in Lesterland, if we Lesters received a letter from the government informing us that we got to pick who was allowed to run in the general election, it's at least *possible* that we Lesters would make that choice in light of (at least our) view of the public good of Lesterland. If Lesterland is like the United States, then the Lesters of Lesterland are black and white, rich and poor. They are no doubt skewed in age (we're older, on average, than the rest of you); they're certainly skewed in sex (I've never met a female Lester). But there's something wonderfully random about the name Lester, which it's at least possible could translate into a fairly random selection of citizens empowered to make this critical electoral decision: who gets to run in the general election.

But in U.S.A.-land, we don't have to speculate about what's "possible." In U.S.A.-land, we know what's real: Our Lesters – the Funders – don't exercise their power to serve the public good. Our Lesters, the Funders, use their power to advance their own private good.

How do we know that? What's the evidence?

My claim is not that none of "the Funders" use their power to advance the public interest. No doubt there are plenty who use their wealth to try to do what they believe is good and right, regardless of how it might affect them.[1] The United States is world famous for the generosity of its rich. Giving $202 billion in 2011, we ranked #1 out of 153 countries studied in the Charities Aid Foundation's World Giving Index; in 1995, Americans "gave, per capita, three and a half times as much to causes and charities as the French, seven times as much as the Germans, and fourteen times as much as the Italians."[2] And, just as a billionaire might give $100 million to fund a cancer wing at a hospital, a billionaire might give $100,000 to a set of candidates for Congress who promise to do something for a cause that is undoubtedly in the public's good, and not at all (especially) in that funder's good.

Consider, for example, my favorite Lester: Arnold Hiatt. As I described in my book *Republic, Lost,* Hiatt was the chairman and president of Stride Rite Corporation. In 1996, he was also the second-largest contributor to the Democratic Party. But his contributions were exclusively to candidates who promised to radically change the power of rich people like him to exercise their influence in elections. Hiatt favored citizen-funded elections in which candidates would draw the resources they need to fund their campaigns from millions of ordinary citizens rather than thousands of Lesters. So, in effect, Hiatt was spending his money to assure that people like him couldn't spend their money to influence politics in the future.

Whether you like what Hiatt was pushing or not, it's pretty clear he wasn't pushing it to advance his own private interests. And, no doubt, there are many others. They have a reasonable conception of "the public good." That is the good they are trying to fund.

But as confident as we can be that there are Lesters like Hiatt, we can be even more confident that there are many more Lesters among the Funders who are exercising their influence to drive public policy in a way that has nothing to do with "the public good."

We can see this point either through anecdotes or through patterns.

By far, the largest contributors to the 2010 congressional elections were people associated with the "financial sector." And among those, there were many from the biggest banks, keen to avoid the regulation of "derivatives." Of the $320 million given by the "financial sector," for example, 40 percent came from the securities industry and commercial banks.[3]

"Derivatives" are the "financial weapons of mass destruction," as Warren Buffet described them in 2002, which in 2008 were largely responsible for the collapse on Wall Street and the subsequent collapse of our economy.[4]

Derivatives were responsible for these collapses in part because the market didn't understand just how exposed the market was to their destabilizing effect. For unlike other important financial instruments – such as stocks and bonds — derivatives are essentially not regulated. And I don't mean "regulated" in the sense of the government setting a price for derivatives, or controlling how many could be sold. Instead, I mean "regulated" in the simple sense of transparency. Thus while a company publicly offering stock typically has to sell that stock on a public exchange, subject to a set of extensive public disclosures and anti-fraud requirements, a company offering a derivative had no obligation to sell that asset on a public exchange, and had no requirement to make any public disclosures about the type or quality of the assets upon which that derivative was derived. The difference between those selling derivatives and those selling stocks was thus the difference between a bookie and a stockbroker. (And remember, in most states, bookies are banned.)

From the perspective of economic efficiency, it's pretty hard to justify this difference in regulatory treatment. Markets are efficient, economists tell us, so long as information within that market is freely and openly shared. More stringently, markets are perfectly efficient only when information is perfectly shared. Of course, that means markets are never perfectly efficient, because information within markets is never perfect. But one critical role of public policy is to push markets toward efficiency — especially with incredibly complicated assets such as derivatives, and especially when the (notional) value of those assets is almost 40 times the total GDP of the United States economy — $600 trillion.[5] The collapse of a market this big could obviously throw an economy off the cliff. It happened in 2008 and it could happen again. So while we don't have a good public reason to force every complex agreement into the public domain (e.g., marriage agreements), we do have a fairly strong public reason to force information about derivatives into the public domain.

But those who sell derivatives are not eager to have that information pushed into the public domain. The more transparent the market is, the greater is the competition. The greater the competition, the easier it is for customers to compete for lower prices. Lower prices means lower profits for the banks and others issuing those derivatives. So to keep their profits high, these special interests seek to keep the market for derivatives obscure.

There are lots of hard cases in public policy. This is not one of them. This is an insanely easy case. The gains to the public in efficiency and stability are huge; the only loss would be to the profits of Wall Street, already among the most profitable sectors in economic history. And as the consequence of those huge profits, in part at least, was the instability of the U.S. economy, it should be pretty simple for policy analysts from both the Left and the Right to conclude that this market too ought to be fundamentally transparent. The issue, to put it simply but perfectly accurately, should be a "no-brainer."

Yet Congress struggles over this "no-brainer" *to this day* precisely because it comes wrapped in millions of dollars in campaign contributions from the very people who are advocating the brain-dead policy. Of course, those special interests are free to advocate as they wish. This is the United States. But there's no doubt about the motive behind their advocacy: It is not the public's interest. As Daniel Patrick Moynihan put it, "Everyone is entitled to his own opinion, but not his own facts."[6] The *fact* is, the push to keep derivatives unregulated is a push to benefit a private interest against the public's.

There are any number of such examples that could be marshaled to make this unremarkable claim — that the Funders of U.S.A.-land use their power to push their own private interest, not the public's interest. (I collect a bunch of them in my book *Republic, Lost.* Read 'em and weep.) But the argument is not just an anecdote. There are plenty of data about patterns as well.

My favorite recent source is a book by a Princeton political scientist, Martin Gilens, *Affluence and Influence* (Princeton 2014), which demonstrates conclusively how policy in the U.S. bends to the attitudes of the most affluent without any demonstration that those favored policies tilt toward the public's good ("when preferences between the well-off and the poor diverge, government policy bears absolutely no relationship to the degree of support or opposition among the poor" and "median-income Americans fare no better"; the "bias, in short, is enormous"[7]). And, likewise, work by Thomas Stratmann shows that even the timing of contributions to candidates has a large impact on the votes by congress-people on quintessentially special-interest legislation.[8] This is just a sample of a growing industry of research tying the real work of Congress to the interests of a few.

So, then, here's the news flash that will surprise literally not one American: He who pays the piper calls the tune — and calls the tune as he likes (as opposed to as "we like"). The influence that is exercised by our Lesters is not, on balance, an influence that's exercised to advance the public interest. In this sense, the United States is worse than Lesterland.

"But aren't the Funders the most successful, the most intelligent, the most hard working of Americans? And shouldn't we want them to have a large role in determining the public's agenda?"

I have endless respect for the rich. Indeed, the most distinctive fact about the rich today is that they do work insanely hard. In 1929,

> 70 percent of the income of the top .01 percent of income earners in the United States came from holdings of capital. ... The rich were truly the idle rich. In 1998, wages and entrepreneurial income made up 80 percent of the income of the top .01 percent.[9]

Today's rich are not idle. And if I could get Larry Page or Jeff Bezos to spend even five hours a week helping to steer the United States in the right direction, I'd gladly pay twice their salary for the privilege. For indeed, properly focused, these icons are icons because they have an incredible ability to figure out how best to direct scarce resources to their chosen end. If their chosen end were the public's end, the public would do quite well.

But my whole point is that when the Funders of U.S.A.-land are exercising their influence, the public's end is normally not "their chosen end." They're instead using the public as one more means to achieve their own private good (and I'm not talking about Page or Bezos here specifically; I'm talking about Funders more generally). Their loyalty is to their stockholders, not the stockholders (aka, citizens) of the United States.

"But aren't there Funders on both the Left and the Right? And don't they simply cancel each other out?"

Of course there are Funders in the Democratic Party and Funders in the Republican Party — and some even more extreme than either the Democratic or the Republican Party.

But even if the number of Funders on each side of the political divide were perfectly equal, it is just a confusion to believe that the fight between the super-rich of the Left and Right exhausts the political issues of America. The Lesters of U.S.A.-land are not a representative sample of U.S.A.-land. Their attitudes and views are not ours.

"This just sounds like class warfare. Isn't that a fight for Europeans, not us? Are we really back to a battle about whether the U.S. should or should not be on the road to ~~serfdom~~ *socialism?"*

Here is the most important point to understand if you're going to understand what the metaphor of Lesterland means:

"The Funders" are not "the rich."

Of course you have to be rich to be a Funder. But "the rich" are not in any sense represented by the Funders either. The vast majority of the rich don't give squat to political candidates. And the vast, vast majority of the rich, especially on the Right, would fundamentally oppose what the Funders in general are pushing: In a code that is most meaningful to people on the Right, and will be more understandable after the argument for the next and third point, "the Funders" are the cronies in the epithet "crony capitalism." They seek the privilege and protection of the government against the challenges of competition or justice. No one whose wealth has come from honest (if lucky) hard work should have any patience with their special pleading. Every one of them should want a world in which the special power of the Funders has been removed. That world will still have rich people. But those rich people will be more respected and honored by the rest of society, because none will believe that they have secured their wealth by securing the special privilege of government.

We Americans don't begrudge the hard working their rewards. We don't even deny the lucky their rewards — as the activist-supermodel Cameron Russell has so powerfully described.[10] What we Americans oppose are rewards from cheating, from bending the system to use the coercive power of the state to make you the winner over your competitors. And the critical fact the rich need to recognize is that, in a world of growing inequality, the basic support for this system depends upon the proportions among these three categories — the hard-working, the lucky, and the corrupt: When America comes to believe the rich are rich because they cheat better, America will no longer be America.

[1]For a while it seemed that Sheldon Adelson, for example, was spending his millions simply to support his view of the public good of supporting Israel. It turned out later, as he suggested, that he was actually also quite interested in assuring a new Justice Department that wouldn't be as eager to pursue, among other things, crimes that he has suggested his company may have committed. M. Allen, "Adelson: Inside the Mind of the Mega-Donor," Politico, Sept. 23, 2012, accessed March 25, 2013 (link #6); and I. Volsky, "GOP's Largest Campaign Contributor Admits to Bribing Foreign Officials," ThinkProgress, accessed March 25, 2013 (link #7).

[2]A.C. Brooks, "A Nation of Givers," The American, March/April 2008, accessed March 25, 2013 (link #8). "Total giving to charitable organizations was $298.42 billion in 2011 (about 2 percent of GDP)." Also see World Giving Index 2011: A Global View of Giving Trends, Charities Aid Foundation, 2011, accessed March 25, 2013 (link #9).

[3]OpenSecrets.org, accessed March 25, 2013 (links #10, 11, 12, and 13).

[4]W. Buffet, "Warren Buffet on Derivatives," summary from Hathaway Annual Report (2002), accessed March 25, 2013 (link #14).

[5]J. Leibenluft, "$596 Trillion!," *Slate*, Oct. 15, 2008, accessed March 25, 2013 (link #15).

[6]WikiQuote, s.v. "Daniel Patrick Moynihan," last modified Nov. 10, 2011, accessed March 25, 2013 (link #16).

[7]M. Gilens, *Affluence and Influence* (Princeton, N.J.: Princeton University Press, 2012), 74, 81 (emphases added). As Gilens summarizes the data:

> The American government does respond to the public's preferences, but that responsiveness is *strongly tilted toward the most affluent citizens*. Indeed, under most circumstances, the preferences of the vast majority of Americans appear to have essentially no impact on which policies the government does or doesn't adopt.

Gilens, at 1 (emphasis added).

[8]T. Stratmann, "Campaign Contributions and Congressional Voting: Does the Timing of Contributions Matter?," *Review of Economics & Statistics* 77 (1995): 127, 135 (studying agricultural subsidies); and T. Stratmann, "The Market for Congressional Votes: Is Timing of Contributions Everything?," 41 J.L. & Econ. 85 (1998): 109-10 ("[T]he date of a legislative event is an important determinant of the timing of contributions … [and] the timing suggests that the motive to influence legislative decisions is important.").

[9]R.G. Rajan and L. Zingales, *Saving Capitalism from the Capitalists* (New York: Crown Business, 2003), 92.

[10]C. Russell, TED Talk, accessed March 25, 2013 (link #17).

Chapter 3:
Corrupt

The United States is Lesterland, point one. The United States is worse than Lesterland, point two. Here's point three:

(3) For the U.S., Lesterland-like government is a "corruption."

"Corruption" is a nasty term, ordinarily applied to very nasty souls. But that sense of "corruption" — referring to the criminal behavior of particular individuals — isn't the only meaning of that term. It's not its most important meaning either. It's certainly not the Framers' primary meaning.[1] And it's emphatically not the sense that I mean here.

When I say "Congress is corrupt," I'm not talking about cash secreted in brown paper bags to members of Congress. I'm not talking about the crimes committed by the likes of Rod Blagojevich or Randy "Duke" Cunningham. Indeed, I'm not talking about the criminal acts of anyone. The corruption I'm talking about isn't illegal corruption. It is *legal* corruption. It's not the bad behavior of bad souls. It's the ordinary behavior of good souls within a corrupted system. The United States Congress is not filled with criminals. The United States Congress is filled with people who have allowed a system of influence to develop that has corrupted the institution they have the honor to serve.

For they have allowed Congress to become corrupted relative to the baseline the Framers had established for how the institution of Congress would function. It's the institution, in other words, that is corrupted, not the individuals — even if it is the individuals who are responsible for that institutional corruption.

We can see that corruption by looking closely at the Framers' design. The Constitution doesn't mention the word "democracy" once. Instead, the Framers gave us a "Republic." But by a "Republic," what they meant, as their writing and rhetoric made clear, was a "representative democracy." And by "representative democracy" what they meant, as Madison explained again in Federalist

52, was a government with a branch (the House of Representatives) that would be "dependent on the people alone."

Alone.

An *exclusive* dependence.

A dependence that, because exclusive, would tilt, they thought, the actions of Congress toward the public's good.

But the whole point of the Lesterland metaphor is to show how our Congress does not have a single dependence. Instead, our Congress has evolved a different dependence. Not a dependence "on the people alone," but a dependence on "the Funders," as well.

This is a dependence too. But it is a different and conflicting dependence from a dependence "on the people alone" so long as "the Funders" are not "the People."

And obviously, they are not. "The Funders" are citizens, no doubt. But they come from a group that 99.9 percent of America could not hope to occupy. They are the tiniest slice of the 1 percent, not randomly selected from the balance of the 99 percent but concentrated and targeted in their aims and influence.

To allow them the position they have in this Republic is a corruption of this Republic. Like a magnet beside a compass, or molasses in a gearbox, or a wheel not aligned, this system of influence corrupts the system of influence the Republic was meant to have. It is, in this very precise sense, a corruption of that system.

There's good news and bad news about this corruption.

The good news is that this is a bipartisan, equal-opportunity sort of corruption. It blocks the Left. It blocks the Right. It blocks both in the sense that it makes it harder (maybe impossible) for either side to get the principled reform that each side would push.

It blocks the Left on a wide range of reforms that we on the Left care about. From climate change (Jim Hansen: "The biggest obstacle to solving global warming is the role of money in politics"[2]), to financial reform, to health care, to food safety, it takes but a tiny number of Americans as

Funders to join together to block these important changes, so long as that tiny number is comprised of Funders exercising the influence this system allows: through money in the money election.

But this corruption also blocks the Right. The Right wants a smaller federal government. But the current system for funding elections only gives members of Congress an interest in keeping a large and invasive government.

For example, when Al Gore was Vice President, his team had an idea for deregulating a significant portion of the telecommunications industry. They took the idea to Capitol Hill. Capitol Hill wasn't impressed. "Hell no," was the response described to me. "If we deregulate these guys, how are we going to raise money from them?"[3]

The need to raise money thus tilts Congress members toward preserving the extortion-like power that only a regulator (or thug) can leverage. You can extort only if your target needs something from you. And a potential Funder has greater needs from Congress the more Congress regulates the things that Funders care about.

This fact therefore biases Congress away from deregulation. That's not to say that Congress never deregulates. Of course it does. It is simply to remark the obvious: The more regulation, the more chains there are for Congress members to pull when Congress members need to raise money. That fact is not lost on congresspeople.

Or think of the Right's desire for a simpler tax system – Herman Cain's call for a "9-9-9 plan," for example, or Rick Perry's call for a 20 percent flat tax.[4]

The motivation here is not hard to understand. The tax code is almost 4,000 pages long. The rulings and regulations interpreting that code would fill a small library. Taxpayers spend billions every year ($163 billion in 2010[5]) just figuring out how to comply with these laws, regulations, and "private" rulings. The practices of tax lawyers and accountants flourish as taxpayers bear this endless burden.

One bit of this complexity is the extraordinary number of exceptions, or "temporary" provisions that riddle the tax code. Provisions granting a special depreciation rate for certain kinds of machinery, or a special tax rate for certain property, or a special tax credit for certain kinds of investments. These temporary provisions are slated to expire after a year or two, and when they expire, the question Congress has to answer is whether that "temporary" provision should be extended.

In December 2010, the Wall Street Journal published a piece that puzzled over the rise in these temporary tax provisions.[6] The "temporary tax code," as the article put it, was a threat to planning and growth. And the "extender mania" that it produced seemed only to be increasing.

So what explained this "mania"?

Surprise, surprise: fundraising! Every time a temporary provision of the tax code is about to expire, there is an easily identified set of corporations and individuals who have an obvious interest in seeing it extended. Those corporations and individuals then become a target of lobbyists who are looking for clients they can represent in Congress to get an extension. As the Institute for Policy Innovation, a right-leaning tax policy think tank, put it, referring to the repeated extensions of the R&D Tax Credit, the first of the "temporary tax provisions" (from 1981!):

> Congress allows the credit to lapse until another short extension is given, preceded of course by a series of fundraisers and speeches about the importance of nurturing innovation. Congress essentially uses this cycle to raise money for re-election, promising industry more predictability the next time around.[7]

So, once again, the existing system for funding campaigns tilts Congress away from a simpler tax system — in part because complexity makes it easier to raise money. And so long as we force members of Congress into this Skinner box of fundraising, they will be reluctant to remove a primary incentive for the Funders to give them money.

In both cases, then — and in many others too — the ideals of the Right are resisted by a system that depends so heavily upon fundraising from a tiny few. That's not to say that if we changed the system of fundraising, the Right would always win. But at least it would be a fair fight. A Congress that depends upon extorting the targets of its regulation to help it fund its campaigns has little interest in reducing the number of targets for its extortion.

Thus, just as the Left suffers because this system blocks it from achieving the reform that it wants, so too does the Right suffer because this system blocks it from achieving the change that it wants. Change, whether from the Left or the Right, is the enemy of this system. The status quo — with all the privileges and immunities that it offers its Lesters, as well as the special incentive it gives the Lesters to fund campaigns — is its friend. In this sense, the current system is a bipartisan, equal-opportunity corruption.

That's the good news — so to speak. The bad news needs no such qualification.

For this system of corruption is a pathological, democracy-destroying corruption. In any system in which members of Congress are dependent upon the tiniest fraction to fund their campaigns, the tiniest fraction of that tiny fraction can use their influence to block reform.

And by tiny, I mean really, really small. We are a nation of 311 million plus. Point-zero-five-percent is a rounding error. And the fraction of the 0.05 percent that's actually necessary to block the vast majority of reform is tinier still. Blocking is simple because there is an economy here — an economy of influence. An economy with lobbyists at the center who sell their services to interests who have something to gain from Washington. Those services are more easily sold the more polarized and dysfunctional Washington is. Thus the worse it is for us, the better that it is for their fundraising.

This is a point that too many miss. There are any number of scholars and pundits who point to the extreme polarization of the current Congress. No doubt they're right. On any measure, our Congress today is more polarized than any Congress since the Civil War.[8]

But the question we need to draw into focus is why they are so polarized.

Certainly, part of the reason is demographics. The United States has changed, creating greater social and political differences than we had before. It used to be that the Democratic Party had real conservatives, and the Republican Party had moderates, and even some liberals. But as the South became more Republican, and the neighborhoods of America became more isolated, these mixed political parties became more pure.

But demographics aren't the only driver in this rise of polarization. Politics — and in particular, the drive to fundraise — is also tightly correlated with this pathology. For the striking fact about American politics is not that it is more polarized, but that it is inconsistently polarized. And the pattern of this inconsistency is perfectly correlated with the incentive to raise money.

For example, most Funders have significant business interests. And at least on big business issues, surprise surprise, we therefore don't actually have Right-wing and Left-wing political parties. Instead, we have two political parties standing right in the middle. Both the Republicans and the Democrats pushed for the deregulation of Wall Street. Both Republicans and Democrats have allowed the oversight of OSHA to wane. Both Republicans and Democrats have permitted the most absurd examples of corporate welfare to flourish — the Export-Import Bank, for example, which subsidizes the financing of U.S. exports, or ethanol subsidies which survived until this year (defended vigorously by Grover Norquist!).[9] Both Republicans and Democrats have voted overwhelmingly to extend the terms of existing copyrights — a policy so obviously against the public's interest that the libertarian Nobel Prize-winning economist Milton Friedman said he would join a brief opposing it only if the words "no brainer" were somewhere in the brief. And both Republicans and Democrats have united to defend U.S. sugar barons who to this day are still protected by import tariffs. As the Cato Institute wrote in 2012 about this policy:

> The big losers from federal sugar programs are U.S. consumers. The Government Accountability Office estimates that U.S. sugar policies cost American consumers about $1.9 billion annually. At the same time, sugar policies have allowed a small group of sugar growers to become wealthy because supply restrictions have given them monopoly power. The GAO found that 42 percent of all sugar subsidies go to just 1 percent of sugar growers. To protect their monopolies, many sugar growers, such as the Fanjul family of Florida, have become influential campaign supporters of many key members of Congress.[10]

Alignment on the money issues thus keeps both parties in the fundraising game. Without alignment, one side would be blown out of the park.

But on social issues, the opinions of the relevant Funders are sharply divided, and the parties naturally polarize to exploit that division. The

Right defends "the sanctity of marriage" against (gay) people who want to commit themselves to everlasting love. The Left defends "the right to choose" against many who see the fetus as deserving of as much protection as "any other person." Framing the issues in this polarized way makes it easier for both sides to rally to engage. And the more who engage, the easier it is to raise money.

"But what about gerrymandering? Doesn't that also increase polarization?"

In an obvious sense, as the deans of congressional studies, Tom Mann and Norm Ornstein, put it, "Redistricting does matter ... by systematically shaping more safe districts for each party."[11] But safe districts also make it easier to raise money, since it's easier to speak to the extremes when you don't need to worry about the moderate middle, and safe seats are, by definition, seats without a moderate middle.

Polarization is thus a scourge on modern government. It has produced a Congress, again in the words of Mann and Ornstein, "more loyal to party than to country." And as a result, we have a "political system ... grievously hobbled at a time when the country faces unusually serious challenges and grave threats."[12]

But here's the punch line that we should not miss: This scourge is a *symptom*, not the *disease*. The disease is the corruption of campaign finance. As Mann and Ornstein rightly put it, that corruption works "in multiple ways to reinforce the partisan polarization at the root of dysfunctional politics."[13]

And this produces the obvious — and what to every citizen should be terrifying — corollary:

What's bad for America might well be good for funding campaigns.

For there are plenty of interests keen to block change. And the more dysfunctional our system becomes, the easier it is for congresspeople and lobbyists to effectively sell the guarantee of no change to those interests.

Most of the time this happens without anyone explicitly describing it. Or naming it. The players know it perfectly well. The less they talk about it, the better it is for everyone.

But sometimes the truth slips, and Lee Fang at The Nation uncovered a wonderful example of just such a slipping truth. The website for the lobbying firm Endgame Strategies promoted its services by explicitly pointing to their ability to leverage the Senate's dysfunction:

> **Managing Holds and Filibusters.** Your organization has an interest in a bill that has proven controversial and you require advocacy before those legislators – often backbench Senate Republicans – who may exercise their prerogatives to delay or obstruct. Endgame Strategies will give you new ways to manage your interests in a legislative environment that gives great power to individual senators.[14]

Dysfunction is profitable, for those who sell it (lobbyists). It becomes a necessity for those who depend upon the help and favor of those who sell it (Congress). Thus there should be no surprise that we have entered a stage in our government's decline in which – except for the random reform-driving-catastrophe – we get no serious or sensible reform on either the Left or the Right.

I n 1846, in his book *On Walden,* Henry David Thoreau wrote this:

> There are a thousand hacking at the branches of evil to one who is striking at the root.

There is a root to this problem. We, as a people, need to recognize this root. We need to see it, and name it, and organize to change it. We all – those of us motivated to engage politically, those of us angry at what our government is or is not doing – have our issue. We all have the cause that we are, in some form, fighting for.

Yet we must all come to see that regardless of the issue, whether on the Right or the Left, reform will get blocked by this one root: this corruption, this dependence upon the Lesters, this dependence upon an influence that conflicts with a dependence "upon the People alone."

"Corruption" is the root at which we all must strike, if we're ever to achieve any progress against the many "branches of evil." Ending this corruption would be the change that would make other change possible.

---

[1]Our framers had a much more subtle sense of "corruption" than we do. Though there was a sense of corruption that described individuals, that was the exception, not the rule. As Lisa Hill describes it, "Corruption was not so much an individualized breach of duties as a condition that spread contagiously and diffusely throughout the polity affecting

leaders and citizens alike." L. Hill, "Adam Smith and the Theme of Corruption," *Review of Politics* 68 (Fall 2006): 636-637. This was also the frame through which Adam Smith thought about the problem. Hill states that "though Smith seems aware of the problem of corruption on an individual level, he sees the issue as more of a systemic problem, focusing almost exclusively on its legalized and normal forms" (p. 650).

[2]J. Hansen, *Storms of My Grandchildren* (New York: Bloomsbury USA, 2009), 59.

[3]Lessig, *Republic, Lost*, 197.

[4]"Herman Cain's 9-9-9 Proposal," Tax Policy Center, accessed March 25, 2013 (link #18); R. Perry, "My Tax and Spending Reform Plan," *Wall Street Journal*, Oct. 25, 2011, accessed March 25, 2013 (link #19).

[5]G. Kessler, "John Boehner's Misfire on the Cost of Tax Compliance," *Washington Post*, Nov. 16, 2011, accessed March 25, 2013 (link #20).

[6]J.D. McKinnon, G. Fields, and L. Saunders, "Temporary Tax Code Puts Nation in Lasting Bind," *Wall Street Journal*, Dec. 14, 2010, accessed March 25, 2013 (link #21).

[7]"An R&D Tax Credit that Works," Institute for Policy Innovation, accessed March 25, 2013 (link #22).

[8]See, e.g., T.E. Mann and N.J. Ornstein, *It's Even Worse than It Looks* (New York: Basic Books, 2012), 45.

[9]See, e.g., S. James, "Ending the Export-Import Bank," Downsizing the Federal Government, Cato Institute, October 2012, accessed March 25, 2013 (link #23); and R. Grim, "Koch Brothers, Grover Norquist Split On Ethanol Subsidies," *Huffington Post*, updated Aug. 13, 2011, accessed March 25, 2013 (link #24).

[10]"Big Sugar Wins in the Senate," Downsizing the Federal Government, Cato Institute, accessed March 25, 2013 (link #25).

[11]Mann and Ornstein, *It's Even Worse than It Looks*, 46. The causal claim made here is contested. See M. Yglesias, "Gerrymandering & Polarization," ThinkProgress, accessed March 25, 2013 (link #26).

[12]Mann and Ornstein, *It's Even Worse than It Looks*, 101.

[13]Ibid., 80.

[14]L. Fang, "Lobbyists Who Profit from Senate Dysfunction Fight Filibuster Reform," *The Nation*, accessed March 25, 2013 (emphasis added) (link #27). The now deleted page can be seen at the Internet Archive, accessed March 25, 2013 (link #28).

Chapter 4:
Known and ignored

We all know this. Everything I've written so far is just a re-minder — a trigger to get you to recollect what you have already recognized a million times over. It is the most ob-vious banality of U.S. political life to observe that the United States gov-ernment is (in this sense at least) corrupt. Not in the Gilded Age sense of corruption, but in a uniquely American sense (that American lobbyists are now frantically working to spread to other democracies across the globe[1]):

Our Congress is corrupt.

It is obvious.

Yet we ignore the obvious.

We ignore it the way we ignore death. Or taxes. Or the end of the world. We ignore it because changing it just seems impossible. The very idea of motivating a political movement to rise up and make this system differ-ent seems beyond the power of any of us. So we turn instead to the prob-lems that seem possible — like eradicating polio from the face of the globe (Bill Gates), or building a database of images of every street across the globe (Google), or developing a truly universal translator of the sort Captain Kirk used to speak to the Klingons and that we could use to speak to the French or Malagasy (Microsoft), or making a fusion reactor in a garage (as Taylor Wilson did at the age of 14[2]). These are the managea-ble problems. They are the possible problems. And so we engage them, and ignore the impossible.

But here's what we must see:

We cannot ignore this corruption anymore. We need a government that works.

Not works for the Left or works for the Right. But works for the citizens of the Left and Right, who bind together to win elections, and then get to see their own brand of reform enacted.

We don't have that government now. The system we have now guarantees that sensible reform from either side will be blocked. So whether it is tax simplification or climate change legislation, smaller government or cheaper health care, financial reform or ending "crony capitalism," this corruption gives opponents the tools to defeat a democratic majority, and to steer the government away from sensible reform.

So grab the issue you care most about, sit it down in front of you, look it straight in the eyes, and explain to it that there will be no Christmas until we fix this corruption. That on none of the most important issues facing this country will we make any progress toward any sensible reform until this corruption ends.

My point is thus not that my issue – this corruption – is the most important issue facing this nation today. It isn't. Your issue is. The issue you care about is. Whether it's climate change or overregulation, financial reform or health care, a complex and invasive tax system or inequality, the debt or education – whatever. You pick the issue. Let that issue be the most important issue that we as a people face.

My issue isn't that most important issue. My issue is just the first issue: the issue we must solve before we can address these other most important issues. Before we have any sensible reform of any one of them.

For we, as a people, cannot afford a future without sensible reform. As Mann and Ornstein put it:

> All of the boastful talk of American exceptionalism cannot obscure the growing sense that the country is squandering its economic future and putting itself at risk because of an inability to govern effectively.[3]

The United States is not the world. And our competitors in the world are not all afflicted with the pathologies of our government. Countries across the planet are able to adopt sensible energy policy, or sensible patent policy, or sensible Internet policy, or sensible health care policy. Those countries therefore do not face the burdens that our economy does – as we pay dearly for a health care system that delivers second-rate health care to too many, as we destroy the promise of the middle class by neglecting public schools, as we choke the entrepreneurial utopia that our country was by selling her future to crony capitalists. It is simply no longer true to say of the United States that we give those who work the hardest the greatest opportunity to advance. We don't. Horatio Alger has moved to Europe.[4] And he won't come home again until we restore a government that works.

---

[1]C. Ho, "Former Sen. Jon Kyl Joins Lobby Shop at Covington," Capital Business Blog, *Washington Post*, March 6, 2013, accessed March 25, 2013 (link #29).

[2]T. Wilson, "Yup, I Built a Nuclear Fusion Reactor," TED Talk, accessed March 25, 2013 (link #30).

[3]Mann and Ornstein, *It's Even Worse than It Looks*, 101.

[4]See, for example, M. Corak, "Chasing the Same Dream, Climbing Different Ladders: Economic Mobility in the United States and Canada" (Economic Mobility Initiative: An Initiative of the Pew Charitable Trusts, 2009), 7. The study ranked the United States 10th in intergenerational mobility out of 12 countries studied and was cited in J.S. Hacker and P. Pierson, *Winner-Take-All Politics* (New York: Simon & Schuster, 2010), 29. See also J.B. Isaacs, "Economic Mobility of Families Across Generations," (Economic Mobility Project: An Initiative of the Pew Charitable Trusts, 2007), 5, accessed March 25, 2013 (link #49) ("Surprisingly, American children from low-income families appear to have less mobility than their counterparts in five northern European countries.").

Chapter 5:
Fixes

So what do we do? How could we end this corruption and make it possible for We the People to move on to the issues that we must finally address sensibly?

The analytics here are not hard.

– IF –

the problem is a system that forces candidates to

(a) spend too much time raising money from

(b) too small a slice of America (aka, "the Funders"),

– THEN –

the solution is a system that

(a) demands less time raising money, and raises its money from

(b) a wider slice of America (aka, "the People").

A solution, in other words, *that spreads out the Funders' influence.* One that keeps a Congress responsive to its Funders, but that makes "the Funders" "the People."

This way of understanding the problem is very different from the way many other reformers talk about the problem. For I focus upon *the effects of campaign fundraising on candidates*, not upon *the effects of campaign spending on the people.*

Others see the problem differently. They say, for instance, that the problem is that we have "too much money in politics," and that therefore we need to "get money out of politics."

I understand this sentiment. I don't understand the analysis. Campaigns cost money, and will always cost money. Yet despite the amount that gets spent on campaigns, we still don't have an overly informed public. We don't even have a sufficiently informed public. And if instead of fundraising from the Lesters, candidates got the money to run their campaigns from the People, it wouldn't be a bad thing if campaigns spent twice as much as they currently do (which would bring campaign spending for an election cycle up to the amount that Procter & Gamble and Verizon spend together each year[1]).

Again: It's not the people who are corrupted by political speech. It's the politicians that are corrupted by the way they raise the money to fund their campaigns.

The same can be said about the view that "money is not speech." That slogan was born in response to the Supreme Court's decision in *Buckley* v. *Valeo* (1976). In that case, the Court upheld limitations on contributions to campaigns, but struck down limitations on "independent expenditures." The Court did so because it viewed spending money to influence political campaigns as constitutionally protected "free speech." If it were not constitutionally protected, the reformers reason, then Congress would be free to limit "independent expenditures" and thereby limit, in their view, political corruption.

That's true. If it were the case that "money is not speech," Congress would be free to limit "independent expenditures." But there would be other consequences too: Congress would also be free to ban any money being spent to influence elections at all, or at least limit it severely — thereby effectively protecting incumbents from their challengers. And depending upon how the Supreme Court sways, Congress might even be free to limit spending to criticize the government, or particular policies of the government, since once again, if money is not speech, then spending money, like any other action, could possibly be regulated.[2]

If I thought that the only way to end the corruption of our government was to risk this type of censorship, I'd think long and hard about whether to risk it.

But I don't think this is the only way to end this corruption. I believe instead that we can change the way candidates fund their campaigns without changing *Buckley* v. *Valeo* in particular, or the way the First Amendment protects free speech generally.

Again: *the problem is not the speech. The problem is the fundraising.*

The same point applies to the view held by some that we could solve this problem of corruption if only "corporations were not 'persons'" and if, therefore, they were denied constitutional rights. That they are "persons" has been the view of a majority on the Supreme Court for some time. Why they are deemed "persons" has been a puzzle for the rest of us for that same "some time."[3]

Yet this view — that corporations being persons is the problem — is mistaken: For the problem as I've described it has nothing to do with whether corporations are persons. Even if they weren't, and therefore had not power to spend money on politics, the Lesters would still be funding the campaigns. And even with corporations as "persons," we can still change the system so that the Funders are not corrupting elections.

That's not to say that I agree with the silly decisions of the Supreme Court restricting the ability of government to regulate in important areas of health and welfare, all in the name of "free speech." (On this reasoning, for example, the courts have struck down a Massachusetts law regulating tobacco companies' marketing to kids, and a Vermont law that required food companies to label genetically modified food.) I don't. I think the Supreme Court is wrong in those cases. And we need to work — especially law professors need to work — to explain to the Court just why.

But we citizens need to recognize that the problem with America's democracy is not just some recent Supreme Court decisions. The problem with America's democracy is America's democracy. The problem is the Skinner box that candidates for Congress must live within just to raise the money they need to run their campaigns. That Skinner box is the corruption. And whatever the virtues in declaring that corporations are not persons, that declaration will not liberate Congress from the box.

Or, finally, some believe that any problem with the current system would be solved simply by more transparency. That somehow, if we could see who gave what more clearly than we already do, we would be less concerned with how the "who" was inspired to give the "what."

This view is also just wrong — not because we don't need transparency in the system. We do. We obviously do.[4] But transparency alone won't solve the corruption of this system, and in the short term, it may well make the problems of trust worse.[5]

My friend David Donnelly, who has been fighting this fight as long as anyone, makes the point beautifully with a perfectly tuned metaphor:

When the Deepwater Horizon undersea oil well exploded and started pouring millions of gallons of oil into the Gulf of Mexico, it was certainly a good thing that we got to see the spewing oil because someone had installed an underwater webcam to view it. But it would be a pretty fundamental confusion to believe that the problem of the Deepwater Horizon would be solved if only we had a better, clearer, maybe HD webcam. Seeing the sludge was good. But to fix the problem means stopping the sludge, not seeing it more clearly.

So too with the corruption of campaign finance: No doubt we need to see who gave what.[6] But we don't inspire people to be engaged in government, or in elections, simply by showing ever more clearly the corrupt influence that money creates. As John R. Hibbing and Elizabeth Theiss-Morse put it, "We should not look to new ways of exposing people to every nook and cranny of the decision-making process as a solution to people's negative views of government."[7] We should look instead to changing the very good reasons people have for this negative view of government. Transparency of course. But not transparency alone.

So again, the analytics are easy: We solve this corruption not by "getting money out of politics," not by declaring that "money is not speech," not by pursuing the "red herring," as Garrett Epps describes it,[8] of declaring that "corporations are not persons," and not just by making every transaction in politics perfectly transparent. We solve this problem by embracing "citizen-funded elections." By adopting a system, in other words, that:

(a) demands less candidate time raising money, and

(b) enables candidates to raise that money from a wider slice of America.

Such a system of "citizen-funded elections" would not require a constitutional amendment, or at least not at first. Even this Supreme Court has clearly affirmed the power of Congress to complement the system for funding elections in a way that would effectively spread the influence of the funders to the people generally. And there are several powerful proposals floating about today that would achieve this effect perfectly well.

In 2010, for example, the House of Representatives came close to passing the *Fair Elections Now Act*, which would give candidates a chance to fund their campaigns with small-dollar contributions only. After qualifying through a large number of small donations, candidates would receive a large lump sum to fund their campaigns, and small contributions ($100 or less) received after qualifying would be matched by the government 5 to 1.[9]

Likewise, the American Anti-Corruption Act, certainly the most comprehensive reform proposal advanced in a century, and supported by Represent.US, would give every voter a $100 voucher, which citizens could then give to candidates who agree to fund their campaign with small-dollar contributions only.[10]

Or again, an idea that I've advanced called the Grant and Franklin Project would have a smaller voucher ($50), funded by rebating the first $50 every voter pays in taxes (and despite what you might have read, every voter certainly sends at least $50 to the federal treasury). Candidates could receive those vouchers if they agree to fund their campaign with vouchers only, plus contributions capped at $100 per citizen.

Or, finally, Congressman John Sarbanes, a fourth-term Democrat from Maryland and certainly among the most important of Congress's reformers, has proposed *The Government By the People Act*, which offers matching grants, tax credits, and a pilot program for vouchers, all to the end of making it feasible for candidates to fund their campaigns with small-dollar contributions only.[11]

Each of these proposals would make it possible for candidates to step out of the Skinner box and return to the task of governing, because each of them would spread the funder influence from the Lesters to the People and change the dynamic of dependence. Each of them has been tried in some form in the states. Each of them could be tinkered with to give candidates an opportunity to run winning elections without ever having to become dependent upon the Lesters, and without ever having to act in a way that draws their integrity into doubt.

Indeed, for me, insanely and overly sensitive as I am, this is among the most important issues that any member of Congress needs to recognize. As one former member explained his decision to leave Congress:

> People just presume we are dishonorable. ... Imagine living under a cloud of suspicion all the time. If you can do that, you can understand why some of us think serving in Congress isn't enjoyable.[12]

For this is among the greatest sins of the current system: No matter what a member of Congress does, there is always the plausible argument that she did it because of the money. Even if the action is at the core of her beliefs, we as a people believe she did it because of the money. The system that Congress has allowed to evolve doesn't allow us to trust Congress. So we don't — which is why America's confidence in Congress hovers at below 15 percent.[13]

But if we change that system by giving Congress members the chance to embrace an alternative of small-dollar funding, then we give them the chance to earn our trust again. Citizen-funded elections would make it (almost) impossible to believe that any Congress did whatever it did "because of the money." Instead, citizen-funded elections would make it possible for all of us to believe — as we desperately want to believe — that whenever Congress did something silly, it was either because there were too many Democrats, or because there were too many Republicans, but not because of the money.

"But what about the SuperPACs? Even if we had 'citizen-funded elections,' won't SuperPACs continue to dominate the system? And won't the Lesters simply turn to them to find a way to exert their influence?"

There's no doubt that *Citizens United* unleashed a series of decisions by courts and the Federal Election Commission (FEC) that have created a new and even more virulent instance of precisely the corruption I've described.[14] Before *Citizens United*, Members were dependent upon the Funders to fund their campaigns. After *Citizens United*, members of Congress are dependent upon the Funders to fund their SuperPACs too. Not technically "their" SuperPACs, of course, because the whole idea of SuperPACs is that they are "independent" of the candidates (and if you believe that, then...). But whether they have "their SuperPAC" or not, candidates for Congress must now inspire the Lesters to contribute to their campaign and to these independent groups too.

The incentives here are truly invidious. As former Senator Evan Bayh (D-IN) once described it to a television reporter, every incumbent in D.C. is now terrified that 30 days before an election, some SuperPAC will drop $1 million in ads against him or her. That fear inspires a logical response: Incumbents seek to secure a kind of SuperPAC insurance – a guarantee that if they are attacked, an equal but opposite response will be launched defending the incumbent. But because the incumbents can't simply turn to their own largest contributors (by definition, these contributors have maxed out), the incumbents must secure that insurance by finding a SuperPAC on their side that has a strong enough reason to intervene to support that incumbent. And all this security has to be in place long before there is an attack. So the incumbent needs to cement the loyalty of this potentially friendly SuperPAC, in just the way SuperPACs like – by voting according to the views supported by the Funders of the SuperPAC.[15]

This is the economics of a protection racket. Long before even a single dollar is spent, the very threat that dollars will be spent has changed the behavior of the government in power. And in this obvious dynamic, the dependence of Congress upon the Funders has been radically increased.

So of course I agree that *Citizens United* is a real problem. And it may well be that we need to amend the Constitution to deal with that real problem. But (1) even if we do, that doesn't change the strategy that we should be following right now. And (2) in any case, I'm not yet convinced that we will in fact have to amend the Constitution to deal with *Citizens United.*

(1)   The need to amend the Constitution eventually doesn't change the strategy now, because the only way we will ever have the political support in Congress to defend an election system of integrity is if we have a Congress chosen through an election system of integrity. We need, in other words, to change the way Congress's elections are funded, if we're to have any chance of achieving the supermajority support that we'd need to change the way the Constitution has been

interpreted. The first step to changing the Constitution is thus to change Congress. But more importantly,

(2) it's not even clear that we need to change the Constitution to deal with *Citizens United.*

First, citizen funding may be enough. As the nonprofit **Dēmos** puts it,

> If candidates for federal office were mostly raising money in small contributions from average citizens, and if outside spending groups were organizing these average citizens to give them a louder voice in the political process, the sheer volume of money raised and spent might not present such a troubling problem.[16]

Even with SuperPACs, this tactic may give members of Congress enough independence to do the right (according to their constituents' view) thing. And that would mean we could ignore this ignoble decision and get on with the project of doing government well.

Second, even if citizen funding is not enough, for complicated law-geek reasons that I've explained elsewhere,[17] it's not even clear that *Citizens United* denies Congress the power to address the most virulent problem that has developed since it was decided – SuperPACs. It's my view that if presented in the right way, the Supreme Court would conclude that SuperPACs can be regulated, because SuperPACs are corruption incarnate (in the sense that I have described in this book).

But even if I'm wrong about that, here is the critical point:

It would be an incredible waste of a reform movement to focus its energy upon reversing a Supreme Court decision – especially a decision that didn't even cause the initial problem.

Citizens United was a close vote. An incredibly close vote. At least two of the justices in that majority are not going to hang on to their seats for much longer. When they step down, at least if they're replaced by more moderate justices, it is difficult to believe that the extremism of that opinion will survive. So why build a movement to demand what time will give us anyway?

Especially because if this is what we fight for, and this is what we get – reversing *Citizens United* – we will not have begun to get what we need to solve the corruption of this system.

For remember: On January 20, 2010, the day before *Citizens United* was decided, our democracy was already broken. The corruption I have described was already flourishing. We have lived in Lesterland for at least 18 years. *Citizens United* didn't take us there. And if all we achieved through this movement of reform is a return to the world that existed on January 20, 2010, we will have achieved nothing.

We need a movement that speaks truth, not trendiness. A movement that teaches America what the problem actually is, and how that problem can be fully fixed. The analytics in that lesson should be clear: We fix this corruption only by freeing candidates from the Skinner box of campaign funding. Anything less than that would be a failure.

---

[1]S. Christ, "Which Companies Spend the Most on Advertising?," accessed March 25, 2013 (link #31).

[2]The qualification "sways" turns upon how the Supreme Court applies its decision in *R.A.V. v. City of St. Paul, Minnesota*, 505 U.S. 377 (1992), in which the Court held that even unprotected speech couldn't be regulated in a viewpoint-based way. But how that principle would apply to something deemed "not speech" is uncertain.

[3]See the extensive and wonderful analysis in Jeffrey D. Clements' *Corporations Are Not People* (San Francisco: Berrett-Koehler Publishers, 2012).

[4]The story of what we need and why is complicated. See L. Lessig, "Against Transparency," *New Republic*, Oct. 9, 2009, accessed March 25, 2013 (link #32).

[5]J.R. Hibbing and E. Theiss-Morse, *Stealth Democracy: Americans' Beliefs about How Government Should Work* (Cambridge: Cambridge University Press, 2002), 214. The authors report a study about the British House of Commons that examined how the views of the Commons changed after debates in the Commons were televised: "For every respondent who claimed his or her view of parliament had improved ... four said it had declined."

Hibbing and Theiss-Morse are skeptical about the good from transparency, and they trace enthusiasm about transparency (naive, in their view) to Jeremy Bentham. As they put it:

> Bentham (1839) supported publicizing every move made by government because such a practice would, among other things, motivate public officials to do their duty. And Bentham believed that those who opposed publicity must assume citizens are incompetent. Neither of these assertions withstands scrutiny.

Hibbing and Theiss-Morse, *Stealth Democracy*, 212.

[6]It is not clear why we need to know who gave what, if we could know what kind of person gave what. So, for instance, as Bruce Cain has proposed, a system of disclosure that would report an amount given and the demographic information of the giver would satisfy legitimate state interests. This view strikes me as correct. See B. Cain, "Shade from the Glare," Cato Unbound, accessed March 25, 2013 (link #33).

[7]Hibbing and Theiss-Morse, *Stealth Democracy*, 213.

[8]G. Epps, *Wrong and Dangerous: Ten Right-Wing Myths about Our Constitution* (Lanham, Md.: Rowman & Littlefield Publishers, 2012), 80. See also page 75: "Reversing 'corporate personhood' won't win the battle against toxic campaign funding." Kent Greenfield puts the point quite well: "Saying corporations are not persons is as irrelevant to constitutional analysis as saying that Tom Brady does not putt well." K. Greenfield, "How to Make *Citizens United* Worse," *Washington Post*, Jan. 19, 2012, accessed March 25, 2013 (link #34).

[9]See Fair Elections Now Act, accessed March 25, 2013 (link #35).

[10]See American Anti-Corruption Act, accessed March 25, 2013 (link #36).

[11]See Grassroots Democracy Act, accessed March 25, 2013 (link #37).

[12]Hibbing and Theiss-Morse, *Stealth Democracy*, 210.

[13]J.M. Jones, "Confidence in U.S. Public Schools at New Low," Gallup, June 20, 2012, accessed March 25, 2013 (link #38).

[14]L. Lessig, "A Reply to Professor Hasen," 126 *Harvard Law Review Forum* 61 (2012), accessed March 25, 2013 (link #39).

[15]There was no need for the Court to create this trouble. As I describe in *Republic, Lost*, pages 238-45, the only issue the Court needed to resolve in that case was whether a nonprofit film company could spend its corporate money to promote its own film. In my view, the answer to that question is simple: yes. But instead, the Court reached that conclusion through an opinion that seems to hold that there's nothing Congress can do to limit corporate influence in public elections. That conclusion, as I explain below, does not follow. Mann and Ornstein recount a similar story in *It's Even Worse than It Looks* (page 79):

> As one Senator said to us, "We have all had experiences like the following: A lobbyist or interest representative will be in my office. He or she will say, 'You know, Americans for a Better America really, really want this amendment passed. And they have more money than God. I don't know what they will do with their money if they don't get what

they want. But they are capable of spending a fortune to make anybody who disappoints them regret it.' " No money has to be spent to get the desired outcome.

[16] Blair and Lioz, *Billion-Dollar Democracy.*

[17] Lessig, "A Reply to Professor Hasen."

Chapter 6:
"Farm leagues"

The analytics are easy.

It's the politics that is hard.

And hard, maybe impossibly hard, all because of a street – K Street, the name we use to refer to the industry of lobbying that now thrives within the beltway of D.C.

"Capitol Hill," in the words of Congressman Jim Cooper, a Democrat from Tennessee who first went to Congress 30 years ago, "has become a farm league for K Street."

Members, staffers, and bureaucrats have an increasingly common business model – a model focused upon their life after government. Their life as lobbyists. Fifty percent of the Senate between 1998 and 2004 left to become lobbyists. Forty-two percent of the House. And as United Republic calculated in 2012, the average salary increase for the 12 Congress members they studied was 1,452 percent.[1]

Such wealth is very different from the way things used to be. Lyndon Johnson was constantly fearful of what life after government would bring. As Robert Caro describes it, "Over and over again he related how once, while he was riding in an elevator in the Capitol, the elevator operator had told him that he had been a congressman."[2] But in a world of hundred-percent, maybe thousand-percent pay increases, there will be very few former congresspeople running elevators. Lobbying for elevator companies perhaps. But running elevators – or any other non-influence-peddling work – no way.

Yet if the reform that I am describing were adopted, then K Street would shrink. Dramatically.

It wouldn't disappear. It shouldn't disappear – lobbyists are essential in any modern democracy. But the lobbyists who would survive would be the policy wonks: those expert in advising about the complex issues that regulation inevitably involves. They wouldn't be the power brokers, or the channels through which campaign cash gets directed. They wouldn't be as valuable to their clients as the lobbyists of today are, and thus they wouldn't be as rich. The economy of lobbying in a reformed D.C. would be radically less lucrative. And so it could no longer afford to give Congress members and staffers and bureaucrats the huge pay increases the current economy does.

So for Congress to adopt the changes that I have described would be for Congress to kill the most lucrative public service retirement package that our nation has known.

How then is it possible, one might fairly ask, to imagine *them* changing *this*?

I get the skepticism. Or pessimism. Or, for some, hopelessness. Taking on this power is not easy. Beating it will be incredibly hard. So I understand the impatience that so often greets the argument for reform: Why talk about a change that just can't happen? Why waste time dreaming for a miracle?

I get it. But I don't buy it.

This problem is solvable. Indeed, if you think back to the problems our parents took on — racism in the 1960s, sexism in the 1970s, and then for us today, homophobia — the problem of corruption seems eminently solvable. Those problems were hard problems. You don't just wake up one day no longer a racist or a sexist. It takes generations of hard work to rip that ugliness from our social DNA.

But the problem I'm talking about is just a problem of incentives. And if we changed those incentives, the corrupting behavior that they produce would change as well. When Connecticut adopted a small-dollar funding system for its representatives and governor, 78 percent of the elected representatives — Democrat and Republican alike — opted into the system in its first year.[3] And that's because, unlike in the case of racism or sexism, politicians don't have a deep desire to continue the humiliating existence of life in a Skinner box. If we gave them a convincing way to do it differently, they would take it. Of course, once they understand the consequences of this different system — for their future, if indeed they see a future on K Street — they might not be eager to see the change enacted. But if we could build a political force powerful enough to force its enactment, the change would stick. A new economy would develop — one less lucrative for lobbyists no doubt, but one more closely dependent "on the people alone."

The challenge is therefore to build that political force — something we, as a people, have not done since the Progressive Era, when both Republicans and Democrats alike demanded that the corruption of that age end.

And just as they achieved their victory then, so too could we: For though we might live in Lesterland, remember even in Lesterland "the people have the ultimate influence over their elected officials."

We still have the power to throw them out, which is what we should do to any politician, whether a Democrat, a Republican, or an Independent, who does not commit to fundamental reform.

The Lesters may not like it. But they have been sloppy. They have left us a way out.

It's time we use it.

---

1 "Congressional Revolving Doors: The Journey from Congress to K Street," Public Citizen's Congress Watch, July 2005, accessed March 27, 2013 (link #50); and Republic Report, accessed March 25, 2013 (link #41).

2 R.A. Caro, *The Years of Lyndon Johnson: The Passage of Power* (New York: Alfred A. Knopf, 2012), 4.

3 L. Lessig, *One Way Forward* (San Francisco: Byliner Inc., 2012), 52.

Chapter 7:
How

In July, 2012, on the cusp of a full-scale presidential campaign, Gallup ran their quadrennial poll asking Americans to rank the top priorities for the next president. Number two on that list – second only to "creating good jobs" – was "reducing corruption in the federal government."[1] Eighty-seven percent of Americans affirmed this as an "extremely" or "very important" goal – beating reducing the deficit, dealing with terrorism, overcoming gridlock, and dealing with global warming.

By "corruption," however, Americans were not thinking of William Jefferson or Tom DeLay. There hadn't been a significant federal political scandal in almost half a decade. Instead, the only corruption-related issue that was anywhere in the popular press in July 2012 was the endless attention the press was giving to the almost endless stream of big money into political campaigns. Americans were being shown again and again that the Funders were in charge. And the more they saw this, the more they became committed to the idea that this corruption had to end.

Yet if you had turned to the websites of either the Obama or Romney campaigns in July 2012 (or, for that matter, at any time during the election cycle), you would have found diddlysquat about "corruption." Absolutely no reference whatsoever to this issue, or its importance. Not even a hint of a policy offered by either presidential candidate about how they were going to address this, the second most pressing issue on the United States' top 10 list. Indeed, according to a researcher I asked to look at the question, this was the first time, as far as we could see, that an issue at the top of Gallup's list was not even mentioned by either major presidential candidate.[2]

It's not hard to understand why neither candidate even mentioned this issue. Even politicians get hypocrisy. Unless the candidate could credibly claim that he would change the system, there was no reason to remind people that he too was part of this corrupt system. Barack Obama had done a pretty good job in 2008 arguing that corruption was indeed the issue we had to address if we were going to address any other issue

(Obama: "if we're not willing to take up that fight, then real change — change that will make a lasting difference in the lives of ordinary Americans — will keep getting blocked by the defenders of the status quo"[3]), but after four years of Obama doing literally nothing to "take up that fight," no one was going to buy his raising that issue again.

This unity among us about the importance of this issue is the basis for hope that we might actually prevail in this fight. Corruption was nowhere on the top 10 list in 2000, or 2004. It made its first appearance in 2008, when it hit number four on the Gallup poll.[4] That it appeared then is not surprising, as Obama had made corruption an issue during the primary and McCain had been railing against it since 2000.

But though the politicians forgot about the issue in 2012, we did not. Its salience has only grown among us, even if the willingness of our "leaders" to "take up that fight" is as shriveled as an overripe prune.

The sole reason this issue has survived is the incredible hard work done by a movement I've watched from the sidelines with admiration but with skepticism.

Born of the embarrassment called *Citizens United*, this movement has brought together literally millions of Americans behind the idea that *Citizens United* must be reversed. We didn't take much convincing: As the *Washington Post* reported soon after the case was decided, 80 percent of Americans polled opposed the decision — higher among Democrats (85 percent), but still high for Republicans (76 percent) and higher still for Independents (81 percent).[5]

But polls don't build movements. People do. And the thousands of Americans working through both new organizations (such as *MoveToAmend.org*) and long-established organizations (Common Cause, People for the American Way, Public Citizen, and U.S. PIRG, among many, many others[6]) achieved incredible success by getting millions to rally around what the polls had reported: that We, the People, wanted a change.

In July 2012, just as Gallup was reporting that "corruption" was our number two concern, a broad coalition of these reform groups delivered to the United States Senate almost 2 million signatures demanding an amendment to overturn the Supreme Court's mistake. And as the coalition's website documents, that movement has now succeeded in getting 11 states and hundreds of towns and cities to pass resolutions demanding a constitutional amendment to overturn this decision.[7]

The critical fact about this movement is that outsiders lead it. No doubt, there are some prominent politicians (Bernie Sanders, Jamie Raskin) and former politicians (Russ Feingold) within it, but the real heroes are the people who are never going to run for anything and who want nothing more from this government than to have it work. People like David Cobb, John Bonifaz, Zephyr Teachout, Jeff Clements — these citizens have spend literally thousands of hours traipsing across the country, speaking to Rotary Clubs or in living rooms, to 10, or 50, or 100 people at a time, convincing fellow citizens to join in the most difficult political struggle that our political system envisions — amending the Constitution.

Their success in turn points to the most important fact about U.S. politics today. If you listened to the chatterati, you'd think the only interesting division in American politics is between the right side and the left side. Between the GOP and the Dems. Between Fox and MSNBC.

But the interesting division in American politics today is not between the left side and the right side, but between the inside and the outside. The inside is the politics of D.C., the life within the Beltway; and the outside is the politics of the rest of the country, the life of the rest of the country.

When you listen to what the inside talks about, or cares about, or deliberates (or, more accurately, feigns deliberating) about, and contrast it to what the outside talks about, or cares about, or deliberates about, you might be reminded of the title of the book by John Gray, at least with a slight remix:

D.C. Is from Mars, We Are from Earth.

We care about "corruption"; they can't even spell the word. We want a government of integrity. They sell sponsorships of political conventions to corporations for millions. We want a government that works. They realize that the easiest way for them to fundraise to stay in power is for gridlock to become a marketable product.

They are from Mars, we are from Earth, and it is time we organize to defeat these Martians. (Where is Orson Wells when you need him?)

This is not the first time that outsiders have done this. Just over a century ago, and after more than 30 years of organizing, the Progressives in the United States finally achieved supermajority support for the idea that politics in the U.S. was corrupted, and that corrupted politics had to change. No doubt, we've seen critical social movements since the Progressives that have focused upon much more important substantive issues — the civil rights movement, the equal rights movement, and now the gay rights movement. But those movements fought bigotry, and bigots have a very different power from the power of the Lesters. The civil and equal rights movements had to change social norms, on the way to changing the law. But the Progressive movement had to take on power directly. And amazingly, if imperfectly, after a generation's fight, they have succeeded.

We have to rebuild that movement today. We have been given the essential tools — the Net, and the capacity it has for facilitating true grassroots organizing. Yet I fear that we today have forgotten the most important feature of that important movement.

We today think of "progressives" as liberals. But they were not. The Progressive movement included both Republicans (remember, Teddy Roosevelt was elected as a Republican) and Democrats. And the key to their success was that they fought as progressives for issues that united the U.S., not issues that divided it. Their target was a broken democracy, and the whole country (save the Anarchists) was united in the view that it needed to fix its democracy by further protecting it from the "corruption" of "special interests."

The lesson that investigative journalists and muckraking novelists had taught the U.S. was that its governments had been deeply corrupt. And what united the wide range of political perspectives that called themselves "progressive" — from Republican Progressives like Robert M. La Follette and Teddy Roosevelt to Democratic Progressives like Woodrow Wilson — was the idea that fixing this broken democracy was the most effective way to taking on that corruption.

The Progressives achieved this unity not through a single national progressive organization. There was not a "United Progressives for America" or "Progressives United" in 1912. Instead, the progressive movement was fundamentally decentralized: There were hundreds of progressive groups organized around dozens of issues, but all in some way acknowledging the central importance of corruption reform. There were Progressives fighting to give women the vote, fighting to force America dry, fighting to establish the right of labor to organize, fighting to end child labor, and fighting to enact monopoly regulation. But each of those groups was also fighting for the fundamental principle that Robert La Follette had announced when he launched the National Progressive Republican League: that better, or more direct democracy would "reduc[e] the power of special interests, eliminat[e] corruption, and elevat[e] the quality of American government."[8] The NPRL platform called for the direct election of senators; the adoption of initiative, referendum, and recall processes in every state; the direct primary for federal elections, including the presidential election; and a corrupt-practices act that would require candidates to disclose their sources of financial support.[9] And by embracing these procedural reforms, "the leaders of the NPRL were granting their fellow progressives permission to be diverse."[10]

I'm not sure why the Progressives organized as they did. I'm not sure whether it was a strategic choice or a practical necessity. There was no Internet in 1905. Neither was there a universal telephone system. Or radio. Or computers driving direct mail marketing. In a world without broadcast technologies, there was little temptation to build the Borg to fight the Borg. Political organizing was peer to peer, by necessity. And as progressives saw the diversity develop, it no doubt became obvious to them too that they needed to feed and nourish this movement of diversity by respecting and encouraging its diversity.

But whatever the reason, the reality was genius. Because no fundamental change has happened in the United States except when the country was united behind it. (Except, of course, the Civil War, but its cost in blood and treasure is not an argument for the other side.) Every fundamental change has happened when the proponents have found a way to unite the country across political divisions. And that act of unification has only ever happened when the proponents of change have found *a way to speak* so that every American has had *a reason to listen.*

By saying this, I am not saying there haven't been important partisan victories in American history too. Of course there have been. And I'm not saying I'm not interested in partisan victories. Of course I am. Partisanship is important and vital and sometimes even fun(ny). But tectonic shifts don't happen in Democratic or Republican drag. They happen when Americans think as Americans. When citizens think as citizens. When we all find a way to step above the partisan divide that feeds ordinary politics and summon to life among ourselves a kind of citizen politics.

So the Progressives (circa 1912), the move to affirm the power of the federal government in the midst of economic crisis (circa 1937) (maybe), the civil rights movement (circa 1965), the equal rights movement (circa 1978) — these were all fundamentally a-partisan movements, at least when they achieved their ultimate success. They were each, in other words, instances in which "We, the People" found a way to speak without using our ordinary spokespersons — ordinary politicians alone. These were outsider political movements, which matured and had their effect once the "common wisdom" they taught moved to the inside.

Of all of these movements, the one that is most instructive for us now is the civil rights movement.

The Civil War gave birth to the civil rights movement. Immediately after the war, the radical Republicans gave it its legal form — through the 13th, 14th, and 15th Amendments, and through the civil rights statutes that tried to summon into being a nation committed to equality.

But very quickly, that dream was quashed by a concerted, essentially terroristic resistance throughout the South, and by an exhausted, somewhat complicit resignation by politicians throughout the North. Slaves who had been freed and who had glimpsed a life of political, civil, and maybe even social equality quickly saw that dream extinguished. And the fight for civil rights fell into a deep if restless sleep for almost a century.

The Supreme Court then kicked that movement awake again by its decision in 1954 to reverse its decision (from 1896) and to hold, finally, and unanimously, that *de jure* racial segregation was unconstitutional. And as blacks and whites began to organize to deliver political victories on top of this judicial victory, strategists for the movement had to think through how best to motivate the American people to demand change.

There were at least two distinctive schools of thought about how to inspire this activism. One we associate today with Malcolm X, though it certainly predates Malcolm X. The way to get people into the streets, this view held, was to make them angry. Violently angry. And the way to make them angry was to remind African-Americans about the betrayals of America since its birth. Anger, and hatred, and separation were the effective means for turning people into the streets, so this view held. And if violence followed, then so be it. For the black oppression of 300 years was already 300 years of violence.

Martin Luther King Jr. is linked to a very different view. "Fiery, demagogic oratory ... urging Negroes to arm themselves,"[11] as King put it, would "reap nothing but grief." It may succeed in bringing a small minority to the streets, but no fundamental reform was going to happen with just 10 percent of America. Instead, what King believed the movement needed was a way to speak so the other side could hear. In particular, a way that Northern whites could hear. And the messages of violence meeting violence, or hatred-induced separation, were not messages that the other side would hear. "We can't solve this problem through retaliatory violence," King taught.[12] Riots would only inspire further oppression, and justified repression (in the eyes of most 1960s whites), since repression is the proper way to respond to violence.

So rather than violence, the movement that King led embraced a message "the white people ... will be more willing to hear"[13]: nonviolence. This was the better "strategy for achieving justice," King told them.[14] In the face of water cannon and attack dogs, civil rights protesters were to become Gandhi. And this simple but profound image spoke a message of justice that the other side could not help but hear.

We stand today at the same place that the civil rights movement did in 1957. The Supreme Court has given our movement a gift. Not the same kind of gift that it gave African-Americans in *Brown v. Board of Education* (and not to suggest that upholding the 14th Amendment 86 years after it was ratified was a "gift"), but a gift nonetheless, because *Citizens United*, like *Brown*, has now inspired a political movement.

But the question we face now is how to develop and articulate that movement. And as with the civil rights movement in 1957, that question invites two very different answers.

On the one hand, we can articulate this movement in a way that divides the United States — that frames this issue in a way that is certain to alienate.

On the other hand, we can articulate this movement in a way that unites America — that frames this issue in a way that can find common ground across the political spectrum.

So far, we have done the first. Though the initial reaction to *Citizens United* was negative across the political spectrum, the political response has tilted strongly to the Left. This frame suggests that the problem with U.S. democracy is the *Citizens United* decision, and that the way to deal with *Citizens United* is to declare that "corporations are not persons," or "money is not speech." The answer, in other words, is to build a movement against corporate America. Against capitalism. The answer is to speak to the 99 percent, and hostage the 1 percent.

As someone from the Left, I get the attraction in this frame. The Supreme Court has developed a truly silly line of authority that is insulating corporations from the most obvious and sensible regulation. That silliness has got to change.

But as someone who grew up on the Right, it is as obvious as snow that this way of framing the issue is only going to divide the country, not unite it. For the salient fact about the U.S. is not "the 99 percent vs. the 1 percent." It is that 80 percent of the 99 percent believe that they are part of the 1 percent — or should be so treated. It's not rich people who gave us the end to the "death tax." It is millions of ordinary people who could never possibly benefit from that gift to the ultra-rich. As a child of the Right, I cannot believe that — dream as liberals might — the United States is going to rise up against the free market. We're not going to rally Kansas to what will be called "socialism." More generally, we're not going to win a fight that depends upon convincing the Right that their most sacred views are just wrong.

Or at least, and more important, there's no reason to have this fight if there's another way to frame this issue that doesn't force people to give up what they (think they) care the most about.

Don't get me wrong: If I believed that the only way to save this Republic was to convince my fellow Americans to give up on "capitalism," I'd be there. The only "-ism" I care about is (small "r") republican-ism, as in the representative democracy our Framers meant to secure for us.

But you don't need to be anti-capitalist to be anti-corruption. And indeed, as theorists such as Luigi Zingales, a libertarian economist from the University of Chicago, have shown us, the corruption I've described is a corruption of both democracy and capitalism – a corruption that people on the Left and the Right should all rally against.

For by "the Funders" I don't mean the capitalists. The vast majority of capitalists have never given a dime to any political campaign. And, as I've already said, I don't mean the rich. Again, the vast majority of the rich have never given a dime to any political campaign. I don't even mean "big business." The vast majority of "big business" enterprises wish only to be free to spend their time worrying about business, not a bunch of lobbyists.

Instead, "the Funders" (or at least the portion of the Funders that I'm attacking in this book) are a small set of those with resources who would use their power to bend politics to protect themselves, or to give themselves special privilege. And as Zingales (co-author of the wonderful book *Saving Capitalism from the Capitalists* (Crown 2003)) nicely reminds us, the most dangerous dynamic in capitalism is the one in which capitalists use their power over politics to protect themselves from the next generation of capitalists. When they use government, that is, to protect themselves from competition.

It is this corruption – what people on the Right call "crony capitalism" – that principled souls on the Right can rally against. (Here's Peter Schweizer: "Crony capitalism is good for those on the inside. And it is lousy for everyone else. But it does provide a hybrid-powered vehicle to sustain a large base of rich campaign contributors with taxpayer money."[5]) And this is the same corruption I have described throughout this book. Crony capitalism blocks reform from the Left. It blocks reform from the Right. It protects oil companies from being forced to pay for their pollution. It protects the invasive and extensive regulation of business so as to preserve a target for fundraising extortion.

We don't need to attack "corporations" to attack this corruption. We need instead a strategy that allows all sides (or at least 80 percent of us) to recognize if not a common end, at least a common enemy. We need allies against this corruption. We don't need a single ideology *über alles.*

When people hear this kind of argument, they also hear something that I am not saying. What they also hear is that we need a single, unifying organization that somehow purports to speak for everyone.

But that's not the strategy. Like the Progressives of a century ago, we need many organizations, each pushing the issues that each cares about, from the political perspective that each care about — but with a recognition of the common enemy that we all share. The strategy is not to pretend that we all agree about everything. We don't. There are real differences between the Right and the Left. But however fierce the differences, there should be no difference about this issue: Just as FDR could stand with Stalin to defeat Hitler without the U.S. embracing the Internationale as the national anthem, so too should our Left and our Right (let's not speculate about which side gets to be FDR, and which Stalin) be able to stand together against this corruption without either side being forced to give up on the other values that each holds dear.

Stand together, not become one. An alliance, not the Borg.

This ought to be easy. But as I've spent the last five years giving literally hundreds of talks about the need for this movement of reform, and engaging with people on all sides of this issue – from Occupiers to Tea Partiers, from Rotary Clubs to JPMorgan – I've been struck by how hard it is. In the middle of a hyper-polarized political system, with political organizations that feed on hate and teach us to hate, with news media that profit the more they can get us to hate ("[i]n a fragmented television and radio world of intense competition for eyeballs and eardrums, sensationalism trumps sensible centrism"[16]), it should not be surprising that a cross-partisan alliance is not obvious to American activists. But I am surprised still.

The clearest example of this resistance is a story I told in the first version of this book (*One Way Forward* (Byliner, 2012)): At a teach-in at Occupy K Street, I implored the Occupiers to invite Tea Partiers to sit down with them. "You may or may not like capitalism," I told them, "but nobody likes 'crony capitalism,' and it is crony capitalism that has corrupted this system of government and given us the misregulation that led to the collapse on Wall Street."

Just after I said that, in a scene that could have been scripted in Hollywood, a man sitting in the front row raised his hand and said, "I was one of the original Tea Partiers, and today I run a site called *Against-CronyCapitalism.org*. I can guarantee you that if you started talking about the corruption from crony capitalism, you'd have thousands of Tea Partiers down here joining with you in this fight."

I thought the argument was obvious, and that the next steps would take care of themselves.

They didn't.

Instead, soon after my speech, a sportswriter for The Nation, Dave Zirin, started tweeting about the speech and then writing about it on his blog. We should not, he instructed, be collaborating with the racists from the Tea Party. It was enough, apparently, for the movement to hang with its own.

But here's the puzzle: Someone in the Occupiers' "We can't talk to the 'racists' of the Tea Party" camp needs to explain to me how Occupiers can speak for "the 99 percent" once we subtract the 10 to 30 percent who call themselves then supporters of the Tea Party or the 40 percent of Americans who call themselves conservatives. Zirin thinks these "numbers actually tell us very little about what ideas hold sway among the mass of people in the United States." But are the Tea Partiers, or the conservatives, just confused? Does the 99 percent slogan depend upon us believing that one-third of the country is suffering from massive false consciousness?

Zirin's concern is important. It grows from a desire to build a "true movement," as he put it. Such substantive movements are built around shared ideals and shared values. The ideals of those of us on the Left ("us") are different from the ideals of those people on the Right ("them"). And if a true substantive movement has to give up talk about its own different values or ideals, then it dies. We need to be able to defend universal health care, even if that isn't something 99 percent agree upon. We need to argue for a more progressive tax rate, even if most Americans don't agree about just how progressive that rate should be. We need to constantly and vigorously remind the country about the harms caused by racism and sexism and homophobia; about the plight of immigrants, whether legal or not; about the hopelessness of the poor in the U.S. — even if the vast majority of Americans wouldn't put those concerns anywhere close to the top. We on the Left need to have our movement, to build and rally our team for the inevitable fight over the substantive policies that government will enact — whether or not we achieve fundamental reform.

And so too on the Right. Tea Partiers and others from the Right want a smaller government. They need to rally their troops against all sorts of do-gooders (like me) who have all sorts of new ideas about how to spend tax dollars. They need to keep their troops in line, and, perhaps more important, they need to avoid alienating their members by confusing them with talk that sounds, well, too liberal. Sure, there are Tea Partiers who would pay attention enough to understand the subtlety of a cross-partisan movement. But there are also Tea Partiers — like Occupiers, and like people on the Left and Right more generally — who have two jobs, or three kids, or a hobby they love, and who are just as likely to skim an email about "Reform" and get furious that someone Not From Their Tribe is mentioned approvingly.

But again, the movement, and the challenge, and the practice that I am describing are different. Our challenge is not to build a movement that coheres around a common set of substantive values. No one's going to convince every conservative to become a liberal, or every liberal to become a conservative.

Our challenge is to build an alliance that can agree about the need for a fundamental change in the system itself. An alliance for constitutional reform. An agreement not about which side should win in a battle between Left and Right, but about the rules that should govern that battle.

Such a movement needs first, as the 27-year-old Israeli activist turned member of parliament, Stav Shaffir, said about the Israeli "social justice protests," a "first line of code": a common plank that each side can stand upon. Together.

Our "first line of code" should be this: corruption. A common recognition that the system itself is broken. And a common understanding that to fix this broken system will require not just a victory in Congress but constitutional — as in fundamental — reform as well.

We did this at least once before. Or at least, or forefathers did. This is the story not of the Declaration of Independence and the war against Britain. It is the story of how that newly independent nation saved itself from almost certain failure. The story, that is, of the framing of our second Constitution (1787) and the rejection of the first (1781).

When people today think about that framing — if indeed they think about it at all — the image is not a celebration of diversity. Seventy-four white men, all basically upper class, all basically elite. Sounds like a very boring party (or a faculty meeting of the Harvard Law School in 1952).

But in fact there was radical disagreement among the framers of our Constitution. There were men in that hall who believed that slavery was just, and there were men in that hall who believed that slavery was the moral abomination of the age. Yet these men, with their radically different views, were able to put aside that disagreement long enough to frame a constitution that gave birth to this Republic because they realized that unless they did, the nation would fail.

There is no difference today between the Tea Partiers and the Occupiers — or between the Left and Right in general — as profound or as important as that fight between the factions who fought about slavery. Nor is our challenge as profound as the one that divided them. They needed to craft a new nation. We need simply to end the corruption of an old and proud government.

If they could do what they did, we should be able to do this.

We are different, we Americans. We have different values and different ideals. But take out a dollar bill and read after me: *E pluribus unum*. Out of the many, one. And out of our many, we need to find "one" in the sense of one common understanding that could lead us on a path to save this Republic.

While we still can.

---

[1]J.M. Jones, "Americans Want Next President to Prioritize Jobs, Corruption," Gallup, July 30, 2012, accessed March 25, 2013 (link #42).

[2]S. Mittal, "Important Voter Issues as Addressed on Presidential Candidate Websites, 1996-2012," Oct. 19, 2012, accessed March 25, 2013 (link #43).

[3]April 2, 2008, Philadelphia. Those of us hopeful that Obama would "take up that fight" were quickly disillusioned when he picked Rahm Emanuel as chief of staff. As Michael Grunwald describes, "Rahm agreed with Obama about the dysfunction of Washington — he called the city 'Fucknutsville' — but he wasn't interested in trying to change the game. He was interested in winning." M. Grunwald, *The New New Deal: The Hidden Story of Change in the Obama Era* (New York: Simon & Schuster, 2012), 90.

[4]Mittal, "Important Voter Issues."

[5]D. Eggen, "Poll: Large Majority Opposes Supreme Court Decision on Campaign Financing," *Washington Post*, Feb. 16, 2010, accessed March 25, 2013 (link #44).

[6]See the list at *united4thepeople.org* (link #45).

[7]Ibid.

[8]W.B. Murphy, "The National Progressive Republican League and the Elusive Quest for Progressive Unity," *Journal of the Gilded Age and Progressive Era* 8 (October 2009): 515, 528.

[9]Ibid., 527.

[10]Ibid., 516.

[11]C. Carson, "The Unfinished Dialogue of Martin Luther King, Jr. and Malcolm X," Souls 7 (Winter 2005): 12, 16.

[12]J.H. Cone, "Martin and Malcolm on Nonviolence and Violence," *Phylon* 49 (Autumn-Winter 2001): 173, 175.

[13]Carson, "The Unfinished Dialogue," 17.

[14]Cone, "Martin and Malcolm," 173, 177.

[15]P. Schweizer, *Throw Them All Out* (New York: Houghton Mifflin Harcourt Trade, 2011), 104.

[16]Mann and Ornstein, *It's Even Worse than It Looks*, 62. As the authors describe, the market pressure toward media polarization is almost irresistible:

The Fox business model is based on securing and maintaining a loyal audience of conservatives eager to hear the same message presented in different ways by different hosts over and over again. MSNBC has adopted the Fox model on the left, in a milder form. (page 60)

CNN has tried multiple business models, but has settled on having regular showdowns pitting ... a bedrock liberal against a bedrock conservative. ... For viewers, there is reinforcement that the only dialogue in the country is between polarized left and right. (pages 60-61)

Chapter 8:
2do@now

So what is to be done now?

This will take work. It will take more than clicking a "Like" button or sending a video to your friends (though it will take that, too). It will take work that brings you out of your ordinary mix, and that gets you to speak or act or engage differently. It will take work. It will be difficult. And it won't happen before the next commercial break.

But this is what we must do: We need to build an outsiders' movement that leverages the power of the Net to take on the power of K Street. Not one group with one massive list, but many groups and many lists, all pushing their own issues, while also pushing corruption too.

The aim of this outsiders' movement must be to lay the groundwork for political entrepreneurs: for the candidates who will finally take up this issue, credibly and believably, and make it a cause that the country can rally around.

But politicians will only raise this issue when We, the People, believe it in our soul, and speak about it every time we utter anything that touches on the political. And that means that there is work to do for all of us as citizens, peer to peer, and as citizens within the different activist groups that we know and support.

My aim in this chapter is thus to map the parts of this outsiders' movement, to identify the range of things that must be done, to give anyone looking for a path a way forward. Not everything on this list is appropriate for everyone. But it is necessary that we see the full range that is needed, for this movement will take many moving parts, eventually finding a common rhythm on the way to defeating a common enemy.

As individuals

The first work is citizen work: to convince citizens that this corruption is a root. To show them, in other words, how the issues that they care about are all affected by this core corruption. And how the issues that they care about could be more effectively addressed – if only this corruption could be removed.

To do this convincing requires work – the peer-to-peer work of one citizen convincing another. The truth here must become common knowledge; the link must be uncontestedly obvious. And such truths are only ever spread by people talking to people. Thirty-second ads on TV don't change the way people think about an issue so fundamental. Three friends raising it, and talking about it, do.

But to find those three friends, we need to recruit an army. And if, for every "thousand hacking at the branches of evil," there is but "one who is striking at the root," that means we need an army of about 300K, engaged in the project of showing everyone else this root, and "striking" it.

We need, in other words, an army of rootstrikers: people of whatever background who believe it their mission to get others to see this root. (Jon Stewart was skeptical of that moniker, and recommended "batmen" instead – obviously a man who doesn't worry about clearing rights.)

Rootstriking is thus a meme. It is also an .org: *rootstrikers.org*. Rootstrikers mobilizes this teaching and provides the resources to recruit the teachers this movement needs to spread the understanding the Republic needs. Obviously, not literally teachers: We'd welcome teachers, but also doctors, and mothers, and banjo players, and managers of Starbucks.

Once these rootstrikers join the .org, the site gives them a string of projects that they can engage in, either on their own or with others, each designed to help spread this recognition. These projects range from the simplest – taking and sharing an anti-corruption pledge, or sharing on Twitter corruption-related stories tied to the #rootstrikers tag – to the most demanding – remixing a presentation someone else gave and presenting it to a group not yet committed.

Each project tries to teach one part of the more complete whole. In one, for example, volunteers ask members of Congress and candidates for Congress to pledge not to become lobbyists once they leave Congress. And in the process of explaining the motivation behind this pledge, the lesson of this corruption is taught.

As people complete these projects, they move up in the organization. As they move up, they help organize others. Already there are a dozen Rootstrikers chapters in colleges and universities across the country. To succeed, we must increase that number by two orders of magnitude.

But this message will not spread in the right way unless it is tied to the cross-partisan recognition described in the last chapter. People need to become comfortable with a certain kind of conversation: one that is confident about a speaker's own political views, but welcoming and encouraging of others.

Such an attitude is perfectly contrary to the models for engagement that we see all around us. From the Huffington Post to the National Review Online to the O'Reilly Factor or almost any show on MSNBC (Hayes is our only hope), the general frame of modern media is snark. From any of those outlets, the rest of the world is framed as crazy. Only "people like us" make sense. And thus it could only ever make sense to hang and work and organize with people like us.

Yet there are organizations trying hard to build such an attitude. On the small scale, one conversation at a time, these organizations push a conversation that explicitly tries to draw together fundamentally different people. That's what *rootstrikers.org* tries to do. It's what Joan Blades, co-founder of *MoveOn.org*, has started with a project called Living Room Conversations, which describes itself as an open-source project to encourage small, informal, and respectful conversations among people with very different views. In January, 2103, she co-hosted a conversation with the co-founder of the Tea Party Patriots, Mark Meckler, about the role of business in government. And likewise, Christopher Phillips has launched an incredible project – The Constitution Café – to reconnect with ordinary citizens about the meaning and future of the constitution. As the website describes it, "Constitution Café is a space in which actual and aspiring Americans grapple with how they would sculpt the United States Constitution if they could start from scratch."[1]

These are precisely the places where rootstriking must happen – not just sponsored or driven by an organization like rootstrikers, but powered by the people who participate and instigate these conversations, independently of our or any one group. Again, the mantra: Not one group, but many; not one organization, but all.

This work is critical. But it doesn't promise any immediate or sexy return. There's no election or ballot or challenge, no flashy media. It doesn't produce a petition with 10 million signatures. It doesn't command the attention of the President or President-wannabes.

But what it does is much more important. It floods a culture with a common meme. A recognition that becomes second nature to all who think about anything related to public policy. It builds a public that can be leveraged to political change, even if the building itself doesn't on its own effect any change. This is the politics of bodysurfing: We prepare slowly but methodically, and then we wait for the wave that makes that work worth it.

As groups

The work among individuals is crucial, but it is partial and incomplete. Just as important is the work among groups — among the tens of thousands of activist groups that are already deployed to change policy. Whether on the Right or Left, these groups have enormous potential. They spend an incredible amount of energy pushing hard in the direction they believe. And their hope, in the end, is to be able to mark their work with a victory for the policy that they fight for.

These groups are not going to be converted to corruption as their cause. Nor should they be. Greenpeace and the Sierra Club do a powerful job of gathering and amplifying the passion that exists throughout our culture for real and sustainable environmental policy. AARP does the same for issues that affect older Americans. (And hey, by the way AARP, thanks for the card, but 50 is not "older Americans.") Unions organize workers to improve their working conditions. The American Conservative Union is the oldest conservative grassroots organization in the nation, drawing together Americans "who are concerned with liberty, personal responsibility, traditional values, and strong national defense." All of these entities have a purpose. Corruption reform is not that purpose. And it is a mistake to believe that changing them to that purpose would make this fight any easier.

Instead, the work we must do within these groups is to convince them not that corruption is their most important issue, but that it is at least number two. And that coalitions of these groups need to commit common resources to pushing this, their second most important issue. Let them all tithe. Let them commit 10 percent of their efforts — whether resources or energy — to advancing this more fundamental fight, and that's enough. That is all the tax this movement needs, but it is crucially important that everyone who would benefit from our success pay their tax.

For think about how much easier the work of any of these groups will be once the corruption I've described has been remedied. When the policy fight over mercury in the air is a fight about the facts first. Not the facts only — no doubt the jobs that will be affected by properly protecting the environment against poisons will weigh in the judgment of any legislator. But that judgment won't be overwhelmed by the Skinner box of campaign fundraising. And if it is not overwhelmed, then maybe the right — meaning the correct — judgment might flourish.

This work is the responsibility of the members of these organizations who are also rootstrikers. The membership must persuade the organization to reform. From the inside, the recognition must be initiated and spread. For only if the organization hears these demands from its own membership will the organization really reform. If there's one thing the 21st century has done to organizations of all types, it is to make them at least potentially more responsive. For this is what technology was built for.

There's a second task for these organizations too — or at least those directly engaged in the project of political reform. All of them must become aware of the needs of this alliance. That doesn't mean, again, giving up their own identity. There will be distinctive parts to this movement, distinctively Left and distinctively Right. But these different parts must all acknowledge a common framework. Again, not the framework of common ends. The framework of a common enemy. And they must then at least complement their own way of presenting the issue with a frame that might include this wider political alliance.

This will take some tough talk. *Move toAmend.org* is a hero in this movement. But we need a *MoveToAmendMoveToAmend.org* (I've got the domain name if anyone's up for this) — to get them to add to the mix of calls at least one that could be embraced by more than the devoted Left. Again, the aim is not "either/or." The aim is "this/and." Fight and organize for the "Corporations are not People" cause, for sure. But add to that mix a corruption cause, so that no one need doubt the potential for these disparate organizations to eventually stand as one alliance.

As candidates

This is, and must be, a movement of outsiders. We need leaders in this movement who are not politicians, and not politician wannabes. We need citizens to see other citizens standing up to reclaim their Republic, and doing something powerful with it.

But we also need insiders. Indeed, we will only ever win once we persuade enough insiders to ratify the demands that we will make by enacting them into law. And so this movement must also find a way to encourage these insiders, and include them. There must be a way that they can signal that they are part of this movement.

For some, that signal is obvious. Let them behave as they would want the political system to allow them to behave. Let them commit, for example, to taking small contributions only. Or refusing to engage the Lesters. Or even openly attacking the Lesters.

I'm not a believer in this strategy, at least not anymore. This is asking existing members of Congress to lay down their weapons and fight for re-election with one arm tied behind their back. I'm not a supporter of unilateral disarmament. The key to winning this fight is to win Congress. And the key to winning Congress is a set of campaigns by wannabe senators and Congress members that could actually win. These campaigns cost real money. Only very rarely will that real money be raised solely in small contributions. The vast majority of candidates who disarm in advance lose — boldly, romantically, unjustly no doubt. But they lose. Buddy "free-to-lead" Roemer, who ran in the 2012 Republican presidential primary, taking no more than $100 from anyone; "Buck for Bob" Overbeek, who ran for Congress in Michigan, taking no more than $1 from anyone; or Doris Haddock (aka "Granny D"), who walked across the country in the name of campaign finance reform and then ran for Senate in New Hampshire in 2004, taking small contributions only — these are our saints. But they are our saints because the political system slaughtered them.

So instead of disarming up front, I support commitment up front. A candidate should be forgiven for the (legal and ethical) tactics his or her campaign will have to engage in to win, so long as he or she makes two critical commitments: First, that he or she will on day one of their service in Congress co-sponsor the kind of reform I have described. Second, that he or she will pledge not to serve as a lobbyist after leaving Congress.

Both are essential. We need to elect people who are committed to changing the system. We need to remove the incentives to back away from that commitment. If 80 percent of Congress were contractually disabled from serving as lobbyists, then it would be infinitely easier to ask Congress to change the way campaigns are funded. And the more we add to the mix of Congress who are committed to this kind of reform, the closer we are to the vote that will actually make this reform law: 218 in the House, and 51 (or maybe 60 depending upon the filibuster) in the Senate.

As "the People"

Among the greatest challenges that we face in solving this problem is the utter lack of authority within U.S. political society. I don't mean power. I mean authority. Eighty percent of Americans believe that every change Congress had made to "reform" the system has actually been made to further protect Congress.[2] People don't trust Congress, so even if Congress came up with the very best possible plan for ending this corruption, we wouldn't buy it because we don't believe them. Congress is not an authority for us, even if it has brutal power over us.

Nor are the media an authority for us. Nor law professors. Nor the million activist organizations trying to rally our support. Nor the church. Nor Hollywood. Nor even Stephen Colbert. (Ok, maybe Colbert.) We live in an age of such deep skepticism that we have no institution capable of offering to us – We, the People – a plan that we would trust.

This is a fundamental problem, and it requires creative thinking. If there's no authority that can at least advise us about what we should do, there's little chance that we'll rally the supermajority it will take to take on the entity with the most power in our political system (even if also the most hated) – K Street and its suplicants.

So we need to build something that might earn our trust, at least enough to encourage us to pay attention. Here is just one idea for how such a thing might be built.

Think about an institution as old as the Republic: the jury. Our tradition gave juries incredible power. The constitution requires that a Grand Jury concur before the federal government is allowed to prosecute anyone. Think of it this way: We, the People, as represented through the Grand Jury, must concur with the government before the government is allowed to prosecute one of us. The same with the Petit Jury, which decides guilt or innocence. Once again: We, the people, as represented through that Petit Jury, must agree with the government before the government is allowed to punish one of us. In both cases, the people are represented in a nonpermanent, amateur body to stand between the citizens and the government, and thereby keep the government in check.

Juries do their work by deliberating. Evidence is presented to them, and then they chew on it and come up with a conclusion. Sometimes those deliberations are constructive; often they are a joke. But the idea behind the jury system is that we entrust this incredible state power — essential to a prosecution, and conviction — to ordinary individuals given a fair chance to hear the evidence and deliberate. That is, we trust amateurs to decide how the professional power of government gets deployed.

There are lots of flaws with the jury system as it has developed. If the jury is really to represent us, it does a pretty poor job. In theory, a small group can represent a large group (think of an opinion poll that can accurately capture the views of millions by speaking only to a thousand). But that small group can't be too small (and 12 is certainly too small), and it must be randomly selected (and juries are miles from a random cross section of the country). So from the standpoint of statistics, the jury is a flawed institution, even if from the standpoint of civics it captures something important about how self-government is supposed to work.

So imagine we fixed the problems with a jury — not for the courts, but for our democracy. Imagine, first, that it was larger — let's say 300 rather than 12, meeting in small groups, then all together — and imagine, second, that it was *actually* randomly selected and representative. And imagine, finally, that we convened such a jury — call it a citizen convention

— and without giving it any actual legal power, we asked it to deliberate about how best to address the corruption that I've described. We would give it evidence and a chance to hear both sides. And then we would let it chew on that evidence and decide what response would work best.

Imagine we did this four or five times, in different regions of the nation, all presented with the same evidence, all given the same opportunity to deliberate.

These conventions would produce some tangible proposals. And though I hail from the elite of the legal academy, I am 100 percent certain that, if constituted correctly, the proposals they would produce would be miles ahead of anything that would come from politicians. Not because politicians are stupid or evil or corrupt. But because politicians are experts in thinking about the special interests they depend upon. And the judgment we need here is one devoid of such special interests.

Tangible, sensible, and, I would also predict, consistent, these proposals could then provide a baseline for reform against which everything else would be measured. Maybe the proposals would be flawed in a particular way. Certainly, politicians or interest groups should be allowed to say why. But if I'm right, and if the work of these different groups cohered on a common core of reform, it would be very hard to convince most that those proposals were wrong. I have no faith in opinion polls about complex issues of governance, and I'd be terrified to have my liberty held in the hands of many of the actual juries that decide defendants' fates. But I have complete faith that a randomly selected and sufficiently large body of ordinary citizens, properly informed, could identify the reforms that would make this Republic work.

We need the authority such a process would produce. To get it would require a statute that established these conventions, protected the delegates (both financially and legally), and forced Congress to consider whatever they propose. I've described the details of such a bill elsewhere.[3] Getting Congress to enact it would be incredibly important to this movement. It would give us a stake and a voice in this debate, a debate that's now dominated by too many who would preserve the status quo.

As funders

Finally, we need to embrace the irony and to recognize this: only big money will defeat the system that big money controls. The campaign to change the way Washington works will be enormously costly. That cost will be borne disproportionately by the wealthiest in our society. And the challenge will be whether we can recruit enough of that wealth to make the fight feasible.

For let's be clear about just how hard this fight will be. If we win, K Street shrinks. It doesn't disappear, but it becomes much smaller. And much less lucrative.

As we get closer to winning, like a wildcat sensing a bear, K Street will respond. Recognizing the threat that this reform presents, it will begin the process of defending itself. Of neutralizing our support, and building the barricades of defense.

We need to be able to fight that defense, and win. That fight will ultimately require votes. But it will immediately require an incredible commitment of cash. To win this fight will require a fund bigger than any we have ever seen in any political campaign. And to construct such a fund will require an unprecedented level of support from – you guessed it – the Lesters.

Of course, not just the Lesters. All of us, too. But even with all of us, the heaviest burden will be borne by those who can afford to carry the most.

The trick here is to make it make sense to commit the resources this fight will need. And to do that, we need to borrow an idea from Kickstarter.

Kickstarter (as I hope and expect you know) is an incredible apparatus for funding art and cultural creativity. It works through a mechanism of contingent commitments. An artist describes a project and names a figure for how much that project will cost. Members of the Kickstarter community then pledge some amount toward that cost. But that pledge is contingent: You only pay if the target is met (within the time set by the project). If the target is met, your credit card gets charged. If it isn't, you get a thank-you email and that's it.

The idea seems simple enough. Its effect has been dramatic. If I asked you to compare the total amount raised by Kickstarter last year to the total amount spent by the National Endowment for the Arts, what would you think the fraction would be, Kickstarter to NEA? Would you guess 10 percent? 20 percent? 80 percent? The answer is more than 100 percent. More money was raised by Kickstarter to support new art — completely voluntarily — than the total budget of the NEA.[4]

We need to do the same with corruption reform. All of us might rationally believe that our government needs this change, yet still do nothing to support that change, because we also rationally believe the fight is too difficult, and the resources too scarce. Even if you're Bill Gates and you come to believe that every cause you're working for would be massively easier if only our government weren't corrupt, still you wouldn't write a check for $10 million to fight that corruption, because $10 million is chump change in that larger fight.

But what if you were Bill Gates and were convinced that 49 others would write that check too? And what if we could then get something comparable at each level of wealth — each calling upon a relatively small number at that level to make relatively large commitments, given their wealth?

Pretty quickly, these numbers add up, and without imagining anyone making a really crazily large commitment. (For example: 50 people @ $10 million plus 1,000 @ $1 million plus 100,000 @ $10,000 plus 1 million @ $100 equals $2.6 billion).

This idea is now being explored by an important new organization founded by Arnold Hiatt (yes the same), called *Fund for the Republic.* The *Fund for the Republic* in the short term will raise money to help feed and grow this nascent reform movement. Not money for itself, but money for other organizations. The *Fund* aims to be a clearinghouse, inspiring and supporting the work this reform movement will take.

But the *Fund* is also thinking about this Kickstarter mechanism — commissioning first an analysis by presidential-level campaigners of what a fight to win this issue would actually cost. And once that number is known, it would devise the mix of commitments necessary to build that bomb.

Call it "Project Irony" (but please keep it secret, or at least don't tell K Street). If it works, then a couple years before the New Hampshire primary, this project would announce that it has a very big bomb – a Super-PAC to end all SuperPACs. That bomb would then be deployed in that election for the purpose of building a Congress committed to reform and electing a president who will assure that they carry through on their commitment.

Political pundits will say that such a campaign could never work. "People don't care about process," these pundits insist. "People care about issues. And campaign finance reform – or even 'corruption' – isn't the sort of issue that people care about."

This view is repeated so often that even I believed it. But it's total malarkey. What's true is that politically active people like issues, or programs. To the politically active, a Bill Clinton State of the Union Address – filled with policy prescription after policy prescription, like a tedious PowerPoint presentation, with every issue drained of its emotion and re-packaged as a simple bullet point – is utopia. To the politically active, choosing a candidate is like mixing paint for the living room: a bit more red or a bit more blue. Politics for them is a debating society writ large.

But the politically active Americans are a tiny slice of America. Most Americans hate politics. They hate arguments about substantive issues. They hate having to pick among the 52 types of political toothpaste that the policy wonks put forward.

Most Americans care, instead, as Hibbing and Theiss-Morse have shown,[5] about process, not substance. Americans hate their government, but that "dissatisfaction ... stems from perceptions of how government goes about its business, not what the government does." And Americans see their government – or at least Congress – as a fundamentally corrupted system. People "believe special interest have hijacked the political process"; they believe "special interests and elected officials ... reap personal gains at the expense of ordinary people like themselves"; and they believe that the "bickering and the lack of productivity" that they see is due to "special interest influence." Not because they believe Congress is filled with criminals. Indeed, ordinary people believe politicians "are knowledgeable and informed." But they also believe them to have been "sucked into a situation in which their self-interest and advantageous position" lead them to behave against the public interest. All of which means that "Americans support reforming the political system ... a great deal" according to the Hibbing/Theiss-Morse data.[6]

Normal politicians (and, more important, their campaign managers) don't notice this about the American people because they're not actually running campaigns that target the American people. They target the small subset of Americans who are politically active. Campaigns target the people they can get to vote for the candidate they're promoting. But most Americans don't vote. And in most elections, the people being targeted are very different from America generally.

Yet if a campaign could bring ordinary Americans back into the political process — at least for the purpose of fixing it — it would have enormous potential. And indeed, this last election showed just that. Jonathan Soros, son of George Soros, launched a SuperPAC that targeted eight Congress members from both parties who were particularly bad from the corruption perspective. That SuperPAC, Friends of Democracy, ran ads that highlighted the way in which those incumbents had caved to special interests. And spending a relatively small amount of money ($2.4 million in all eight races), it helped defeat seven of the eight. By the end of that campaign, voters in those districts ranked addressing corruption as the most important issue, and three-fourths of the voters urgently wanted Congress to address the issue of money in politics. Speak to the country credibly about what all of the country cares about, and voters will respond.

But for this strategy to work, the campaign would need a leader. A candidate for President who made this his or her issue. A candidate who was credible and who would win. So who could that candidate be?

If it's an ordinary politician, then as a Democrat — hard as this is for me to confess — it may be that only Nixon can go to China. It may be, that is, that it will take a Republican to make this his or her issue, if indeed this issue has any hope of passing our Congress. While Democrats and Republicans are equally guilty of the sin that this corruption is, Democrats have taken the lead in pushing the reform that would end this corruption. Yet if fundamental reform requires a cross-partisan movement (as I certainly believe it does), ironically, the Democrats will only ever be able to deliver on their reform promise if there's a Republican at the top who is making the case for them. For some reason, "fairness" and "equality" and a "fight against corruption" sound less scary to most Americans when uttered from the Right. Call it poetic injustice if you must. I call it reality.

But it might be that the best strategy is for a non-politician, or at least a very unique politician, to run — not to be an ordinary President. Instead, he or she would be a Trustee, or what I've called a Regent President. In *Republic, Lost*, I describe the Regent Presidency — the idea of a candidate who promises, if elected, to do one thing, and then resign. That one thing would be this reform: to ride to victory on the promise to end this corruption; to stay in power long enough to force Congress to ratify that victory by enacting laws that will end this corruption; and then, Cincinnatus-like, to resign, and return to private life.

This felt like a crazy idea when I first wrote it — more made for Hollywood than made for D.C. But in fact, in other countries at least, just such a reform has occurred. In Georgia, for example — the Republic, not the State — the prime minister in 2012 was someone who a year before was completely unknown in Georgian politics. He was a billionaire, someone enormously successful in business. But he was a recluse billionaire, living in a Georgian village, disengaged from public life. Then, last year, he became convinced that the current president (someone he had supported) was evolving into something of a dictator. But he announced that he would help build an opposition party and run that coalition against the president's party in the 2012 elections. And here was the key: He promised that if he won, he would be a temporary prime minister, serving only as long as necessary to assure that the evolution to dictatorship was avoided. His party won overwhelmingly. The current president accepted his fate. And Georgia may well be on the way to establishing the first real democracy in the post-Soviet era.

The United States is not Georgia. Yet the key in this story is not specific to Georgia. It is a point about how people respond to a clear promise of credible change. People care about their democracy. They don't know what the Fed does, or how many senators there are from each state. But they want a government that works. And most of all they want to believe their government is not being sold to the highest bidder. Those people respond to credible campaigns for reform – everywhere.

Of course, we've had "reformer" after "reformer" in U.S. politics. Everyone promises "change." And most with any perspective on this battle recognize that "change" is just an election slogan. Most see that once a party gets in power, there are too many distractions to keep them focused on this nebulous idea of reform.

But if a President were to be measured on one dimension only – if there were just a single standard for knowing whether he or she had succeeded – it would make it incredibly difficult for the President to not "take up that fight," and give it her all. And that in turn would make it easier for the rest of us to believe that this was a fight worth waging. This is why he or she must resign after achieving the change promised: it makes the promise believable. And if tied to a large enough catalyst fund, if led by credible enough leader, it might just be possible for Americans to pull together the energy they need to make this a campaign we could win.

This, at least, is what we must do if we're to try. Small change hasn't gone anywhere. Reformers have been tinkering for 30 years, but the problems have only gotten worse. That's because reform like this needs escape velocity. Kickstarting a catalyst fund might produce precisely enough energy to get such a movement for real reform off the ground.

---

[1]See Constitution Café description, accessed March 25, 2013 (link #46).

[2]R. Faucheux, "U.S. Voters: Congress Is Selfish About Campaign Finance," *Atlantic*, July 16, 2012, accessed March 25, 2013 (link #51).

[3]L. Lessig, "A Proposal to Convene a Series of Citizen Conventions,' for Proposing Amendments to the Constitution," testimony before Senate Judiciary Committee, July 24, 2012, accessed March 25, 2013 (link #47).

[4]C. Franzen, "Kickstarter Expects to Provide More Funding to the Arts than NEA," Talking Points Memo, Feb. 24, 2012, accessed March 25, 2013 (link #48). The actual results exceeded NEA's budget by 75 percent (see link #52).

[5]Hibbing and Theiss-Morse, *Stealth Democracy*.

[6]Quotes in this paragraph at ibid., at 35, 105, 124, 88. This approach also helps explain the relatively strong view Americans have of the Court. See page 158.

Conclusion:
Possible

Yet still, in the end, no matter how hard anyone tries, most people remain in the place where this book began: Change, they believe, is not possible. Indeed, 91% of Americans believe, according to a poll we conducted at the end of 2013, that the influence of money in politics can't be reduced. Especially the pundits and politicians, and especially people inside the Beltway. "You have no idea how powerful K Street is," I was told by one such insider. "You have no idea how hard it is to build a grassroots, political movement," said another.

Yet the more I've thought about this issue, and talked about it in literally hundreds of venues across the country, the more I've come to think that whether it is "possible" or not is just not relevant.

I first saw this irrelevance in an exchange I described in my book, *Republic, Lost*. After a lecture at Dartmouth, a woman in the audience said, "What's the point? It all seems so hopeless."

When she said this, I scrambled. I tried to find a way to respond to that hopelessness. What hit me was an image of my (then) six-year-old son. I imagined a doctor coming to me and saying, "Your son has terminal brain cancer, and there's nothing you can do."

And I thought, would I do nothing? Would I just accept it? Would I give up?

Think about that for a second. Take the image of a person you love most, and imagine the scenario I did. And then ask yourself, would you do nothing?

You would not. You would not give up. You would do everything you could to save that person's life.

We do this because this is what love means. That the odds are irrelevant, and that you do whatever the hell you can, the odds be damned.

And then, in that Dartmouth lecture hall, I saw the obvious link: because even we liberals love this country. And so when the pundits and the politicians say that change is impossible, what this love of country says back is that is just irrelevant. We lose something dear, something every one of us cherishes, if we lose this Republic. And so we act, with everything we can, we act out of love, to prove these pundits wrong.

So here's the question for you: Do you have that love?

Because if you do, then what the hell are you — what the hell are we — doing about it? For it? And for this Republic?

hen Ben Franklin was carried from the constitutional convention in September of 1787, he was stopped by a woman on the streets of Philadelphia and asked, "Well, Doctor, what have we got?" Franklin replied, "A Republic, if you can keep it."[1]

A Republic.

A representative democracy.

A government "dependent upon the People alone."

Alone.

We have lost that Republic. And now all of us must act to get it back. Through love, and through the terrifying political force that the People, at least sometimes, can muster.

---

[1] W. Isaacson, *Benjamin Franklin: An American Life* (New York: Simon & Schuster, 2004), 459.

Appendix:
Great .orgs

As I've argued, this isn't a movement with a single leader. Nor should it be. There are many in this movement, and many in it for many years. Some, like Democracy21, are traditional, inside-the-beltway reform organizations. But there are many more keen to engage a wider audience in this reform movement. Here are some of the leaders. You can find the URLs for the groups at *lesterland.lessig.org/groups*.

Transparency: Groups focused on making the data about influence more accessible

> MapLight
> National Institute on Money in State Politics
> OpenSecrets.org
> The Sunlight Foundation

Funding: Groups focused primarily on organizing to change the way elections are funded

> 99Rise
> Americans for Campaign Reform
> Campaign Finance Institute
> Common Cause
> Democracy Matters
> Dēmos
> Friends of Democracy
> People for the American Way
> Public Campaign
> Public Citizen
> Represent.US
> Rootstrikers
> The Other 98%
> United Republic
> U.S. PIRG

Amendment: Groups pushing for a constitutional amendment

United for the People
Common Cause
Free Speech for People
Move to Amend
People for the American Way
Public Citizen
The Other 98%

Thanks

This book is an experiment. After giving my TED talk, I was inundated with kindness but with questions. How could we bring about the change that I said we needed? Who would lead it? What would it take?

The brilliance of TED is that it introduces ideas, and thereby enables them to spread. But in 18 minutes, one can only explain so much. So I wanted in this short book to take the framework of my TED talk and fill in some of the details.

The ideas in my talk and in this book have been developed over the past five years. The foundation is *Republic, Lost: How Money Corrupts Congress – And a Plan to Stop It* (Twelve, 2011), and I was grateful that Twelve allowed me the first version of an experiment like this when Byliner Inc. published my e-book *One Way Forward: The Outsider's Guide to Fixing the Republic* (2012).

One Way Forward, like this book, was a map of what we should do, circa 2012. This book is version two of that map. It includes parts from that original plan, updated to respond to changes in the political landscape and reframed as my thinking has evolved.

I am especially grateful to Chris Anderson for allowing and then encouraging this experiment. The staff of TED Books has been phenomenally helpful in producing the original version of work.

I am endlessly grateful as well to my agent, Amanda Urban, for doing what she does better than anyone in the world: helping me think through the next stage in the life of writing.

I am grateful too to the incredible Center for Responsive Politics (*opensecrets.org*) for help with the numbers. Also to Ming Cheung, Sandra Hanian, Alex Harris, Sonal Mittal, Nathan Reeves, Kyle Schneider, Steve Shaw, Matt Shuham, and especially Michael Pierce for research support. Anthony Welch helped me navigate the work of Dr. King. And endless thanks to Ari Borensztein, for both research and everything-else support.

The most, as always, however, is to my partner and lover, who is too often left with the burden of my work done elsewhere. To Bettina, everything is dedicated.

Afterword

After almost 7 years thinking and talking about this issue, I am convinced that the central allegory of this book is the right way to understand just what's wrong with America's democracy today. We have allowed a second election to emerge and dominate — an election within which the vast majority of Americans can't hope to compete, and an election that has convinced most Americans that their participation in the election within which they can compete in the end doesn't really matter. Boss Tweed famously said, "I don't care who does the electing, so long as I get to do the nominating." That lesson has been learned again.

But the weakness in this allegory is that it frames the issue as one of interest. The essential argument is about what we, politically, want: If you care about climate change, or the debt, or health care reform, or a simpler tax system, then you should want the reforms I've described, because without them, you won't get what you want.

Yet the most compelling political arguments are not about interest. They're about principle. They're not about what I want. They're about what ought to be. And as friends have pushed me to frame this argument as a matter of right, and not just want, I've seen more clearly the obvious parallel that deserves much more than the note this book originally gave it. (Thanks to Katie and Szelena for pushing me in this.)

For as one friend put it, however compelling Lesterland is as an allegory, there's something unreal about it shape — until one remembers that for many years, African Americans in parts of the South actually lived in a version of Lesterland.

Until 1944, states in the south, dominated by the Democratic Party, explicitly excluded blacks from voting in the Democratic Primary. As that primary was the only competitive race in these states, that exclusion removed blacks from the only contest that would matter. That exclusion was obviously not a choice of blacks — they didn't choose whether they were white or not. It was a distinction forced upon them, which denied them equal dignity within a democratic system.

That loss is similar to the loss we suffer in Lesterland. No doubt that loss was greater, since the exclusion it evinced within the Old South went far beyond elections. But still, it shares with Lesterland this fundamental flaw: That a characteristic that citizens don't choose denies those citizens equal dignity within the election system.

The difference, of course, is that in the Old South, the vast majority of citizens had the right to participate in the exclusive election, while in Lesterland, the vast majority of Americans are excluded. 99.95% of us are denied the chance to participate in this critical and determinative election, while a minority was denied the chance to participate in the white primary.

Of all the facts that give me hope, in the end, this gives me the greatest hope. For if we can get Americans to see the nature of this injustice, the denial of equal citizenship, then we easily, still, have the power to remedy it.

Not just because it would give us what we, politically, want, whether we're from the Right or the Left. But also, and most importantly, because it would achieve a justice that is now denied to us.

It would move us, as we always and only can move, to "a more perfect union," no doubt leaving many other critical problems to be solved. Still. But with the capacity to address those problems, as any democracy should: with equal citizens granted an equal franchise within a fair and competitive political system.

Brookline, MA
February 2014

Index

About the Author

Lawrence Lessig is the Roy L. Furman Professor of Law and Leadership at Harvard Law School, and director of the Edmond J. Safra Center for Ethics at Harvard University.

He clerked for Judge Richard Posner on the 7th Circuit Court of Appeals and Justice Antonin Scalia on the United States Supreme Court. Lessig serves on the Board of the AXA Research Fund, and is an emeritus member of the board of Creative Commons. He serves on the advisory board of Democracy Café and the Sunlight Foundation. He is a Member of the American Academy of Arts and Sciences and the American Philosophical Association, and has received numerous awards, including the Free Software Foundation's Freedom Award, and was named one of Scientific American's Top 50 Visionaries.

Lessig holds a BA in economics and a BS in management from the University of Pennsylvania, an MA in philosophy from Cambridge, and a JD from Yale.

17518800R00054

Made in the USA
Middletown, DE
28 January 2015